MW01007633

"Melanie Springer Moc... heartfelt exploration of ... parent and teacher of y... parent of young adults o... who is looking ahead to young adulthood, and to all those who teach, mentor, and guide young adults. It is an invitation to accompany young adults in these challenging times—and in the process to learn more about ourselves on the journey of life. You will discover, as I did, the deep sense of hope that permeates Melanie's stories and insights as she relates the struggle and pain, the discovery and joy that are part of the young adult experience."

—**JOHN ROBERTO**, president of Lifelong Faith Associates and author of *Lifelong Faith: Formation for All Ages and Generations*

"*Finding Our Way Forward* is a gentle, challenging, and beautiful guide for parents in a vulnerable season of walking alongside their Gen Z young adults in a culture equally as fragile. As a professor of young adults and a mom, Melanie Springer Mock provides a perspective and voice as a trusted friend who encourages you to love your child while also opening your hands to let them grow into the adult they are becoming. This book is a must-read for any parent of today's youth."

—**BRENDA L. YODER**, Licensed Mental Health Counselor, school counselor, and author of *Fledge: Launching Your Kids without Losing Your Mind*

"Rare is the book that challenges, equips, and encourages the parents of emerging young adults. This is that book. In helping parents acknowledge, then release, their biases and self-informed opinions about who their children should be, Springer Mock offers the invitation to love and celebrate children for who they are . . . image bearers entrusted to our care for a short time. This book is a must-read for any and all people relating to and interacting with late adolescents and young adults."

—**DR. DOREEN DODGEN-MAGEE**, psychologist, author, mom, and neighbor

"Parenting doesn't screech to a halt when one's children become adults. In this book, Melanie Springer Mock offers an honest look at how parents can nurture faith and support spirituality in their young adult children. By weaving Christian theology with stories from her own life, she has created an engaging book that covers a wide spectrum of topics. You will laugh and cry as you join Springer Mock in finding your way forward in a new phase of family life."

—**DAVID M. CSINOS**, associate professor of practical theology at Atlantic School of Theology and founder of Faith Forward

"For all the parents who worry and wonder and wait as their adolescents wander toward adulthood, this book is the guide to help you rest and trust. Melanie Springer Mock's hard-earned wisdom as a parent and educator is a gift to us all."

—**AMY JULIA BECKER**, author of *To Be Made Well: An Invitation to Wholeness, Healing, and Hope*

"*Finding Our Way Forward* is indeed a most spacious book in terms of discerning God's calling. Melanie Springer Mock's words drip with wisdom that we all need, not just young adults. This book is full of reminders of the goodness and graciousness of God as we co-create a life together and a life lived on behalf of others, not just ourselves. God's desires for us correspond not with worldly empire, but with the kingdom. Springer Mock's wisdom is refreshing in an age captured by the myth of progress and seemingly boundless material prosperity for some. We may have to unlearn some things we have been taught regarding discernment and calling in order to discern well—and in that, Springer Mock is a spectacular teacher and guide."

—**MARLENA GRAVES**, author of *The Way Up Is Down: Becoming Yourself by Forgetting Yourself*

"Timely and searingly honest, *Finding Our Way Forward* is a gift for those of us who have raised (or are otherwise in close relationship with) young adults. Springer Mock tells her own 'emptying the nest' story, with all its attendant loneliness, grief, and uncertainty. While she admits that we are all out of our league as we walk alongside our grown children in these unprecedented times, the wisdom and spiritual insight she offers in this book deliver valuable comfort and support. What a powerhouse of a book!"

—**JENNIFER GRANT**, author of *Dimming the Day* and *When Did Everybody Else Get So Old?*

Finding Our Way Forward

Finding Our Way Forward

When the Children We Love Become Adults

MELANIE SPRINGER MOCK

HERALD PRESS

P R E S S

Harrisonburg, Virginia

Herald Press
PO Box 866, Harrisonburg, Virginia 22803
www.HeraldPress.com

Names: Springer Mock, Melanie, author.
Title: Finding our way forward : when the children we love become adults /
    Melanie Springer Mock.
Description: Harrisonburg, Virginia : Herald Press, [2023] | Includes bibliographical
    references.
Identifiers: LCCN 2022047533 (print) | LCCN 2022047534 (ebook) | ISBN
    9781513810591 (paper) | ISBN 9781513810607 (h/c) | ISBN 9781513810614 (ebook)
Subjects: LCSH: Christian teenagers—Religious life. | Parenting—Religious aspects—
    Christianity. | Church work with teenagers. | Adolescence—Religious aspects. |
    BISAC: RELIGION / Christian Living / Family & Relationships | RELIGION /
    Christian Living / Parenting
Classification: LCC BV4531.3 .S695 2023 (print) | LCC BV4531.3 (ebook) |
    DDC 248.8/3—dc23/eng/20221207
LC record available at https://lccn.loc.gov/2022047533
LC ebook record available at https://lccn.loc.gov/2022047534

Study guides are available for many Herald Press titles at www.HeraldPress.com.

FINDING OUR WAY FORWARD
© 2023 by Melanie Springer Mock
Released by Herald Press, Harrisonburg, Virginia 22803. 800-245-7894.
    All rights reserved.
Library of Congress Control Number: 2022047533
International Standard Book Number: 978-1-5138-1059-1 (paperback);
    978-1-5138-1060-7 (hardcover); 978-1-5138-1061-4 (ebook)
Printed in United States of America
Cover and interior design by Merrill Miller

All rights reserved. This publication may not be reproduced, stored in a retrieval system, or transmitted in whole or in part, in any form, by any means, electronic, mechanical, photocopying, recording or otherwise without prior permission of the copyright owners.

All scripture quotations, unless otherwise indicated, are taken from the Holy Bible, New International Version®, NIV®. Copyright © 1973, 1978, 1984, 2011 by Biblica, Inc.® Used by permission of Zondervan. All rights reserved worldwide. www.Zondervan.com. The "NIV" and "New International Version" are trademarks registered in the United States Patent and Trademark Office by Biblica, Inc.®

    Scripture quotations marked (ESV) are from the ESV® Bible (The Holy Bible, English Standard Version®), Copyright © 2001 by Crossway, a publishing ministry of Good News Publishers. Used by permission. All rights reserved.

    Scripture quotations marked (NRSVue) are taken from the New Revised Standard Version Updated Edition. Copyright © 2021 National Council of Churches of Christ in the United States of America. Used by permission. All rights reserved worldwide.

27 26 25 24 23   10 9 8 7 6 5 4 3 2 1

For Benjamin and Samuel
Your love is a gift

CONTENTS

Foreword

In early winter of 2020, I began to stress about how some family dynamics might play out at my son's high school graduation—that coming May.

As I prayed about this (as well as about my own anxiety, which was popping up with alarming frequency), I sensed God saying, *It's not going to matter.*

At the time, I took this to mean that my worry was ridiculous or premature—as so many of my anxieties were (and still are!).

Of course, months later, when graduation (and prom and senior ditch day and senior picnic and final band concerts and so much more) was canceled, I looked back on those words much, much differently. Don't get me wrong: I don't believe God was giving me special insight into the forthcoming pandemic.

Instead, I believe God was giving me the words I would take *with* me into the pandemic and the words that I—like so many of us—would emerge with.

Alongside all the harm that COVID-19 brought with it, all the death and all the suffering, all the losses and missed opportunities, COVID also gave a few gifts. We slowed down. We learned to live without. We spent time together. We ate outside. And we learned that so much of what we think matters—just doesn't. At least, not in the way we think it should.

COVID forced so many of us to reconsider hopes, goals, and expectations for our own lives—and for those of us who are parents, that of our kids.

It's always been difficult to come of age. But for Gen Z— this generation of teens and young adults who have already had to navigate terrain that didn't exist for most of human civilization (hello, social media!), who have access to more information (for good and for bad) than has ever been accessible before, and for whom fear of being shot and killed at school is perfectly reasonable—coming of age, without normal rites of passage, with a world in flux, has certainly proved harder than it was for my generation (Gen X) or even the millennial generation that followed.

Despite the difficulties, however, this Gen Z generation continues to astound me—with their commitment to justice, to reducing gun violence, to goodness, to inclusion, to kindness. I've said on more than one occasion that this generation will save the world. And I mean it. They're on track to figure out the things that previous generations have failed them on. As long as we're willing to heed space.

Because of all this, I'm so grateful that Melanie Springer Mock has written this book. *Finding Our Way Forward* offers young adult parents like me the opportunity not only to reflect on and go deeper into the lessons we've learned from COVID. It also offers insights into raising kids and parenting young adults that I wish I'd always known.

This book is perfect for our time. It's perfect for parents and anyone else who loves young people and takes seriously our responsibility to help them grow into and live as the people God made them to be. But this book isn't about us older folks teaching or guiding. Instead, rightly, *Finding Our Way Forward* is about listening, about lamenting, about encouraging, about respecting. And in another personal gift to me (and, I believe, all readers), it's a poignant book about mercy and humility.

Consider what Melanie says about both:

> Mercy is allowing our children to craft their own life stories, ones that bear witness to their fearful, wonderful, unique selves. Mercy is refusing to make assumptions about the stories they are writing. Mercy is listening to their stories with open hearts and minds. And mercy means letting them make mistakes as they figure out who they are. Because they will make mistakes, and we will too. (p. 133)

> Walking humbly with God requires embracing an impulse of faith, choosing an open-hearted acceptance of others even when that could mean relinquishing our visions about what lifelong relationships with young people might look like. (p. 118–19)

These passages reflect the wisdom and warmth, the goodness and godliness, of Melanie's words in these pages. Indeed, that Melanie writes as both a mother of young adults *and* a college professor offers a perspective I didn't realize I needed. Her thorough research and vulnerably shared firsthand knowledge form a near-perfect primer for those of us trying to navigate these tricky parenting waters. Her words promise to prepare this generation that has already been through so much to lead the way into an amazing future where the things that *do* matter *will*.

—Caryn Rivadeneira
Author of *Saints of Feather and Fang: How the Animals We Love and Fear Connect Us to God*

Introduction

Oregon was on fire.

September winds had blown down power lines, sparking flames in underbrush tinder-dry from a summer with no rain. We'd experienced smoky skies before, from forest fires in mountain ranges fifty or sixty miles away—or sometimes even in another state entirely. But this conflagration was different, because we could see the blazing forest for ourselves.

My Tuesday night class was just finishing when my son Benjamin called to tell me about the nearby fire. "I think Grandma and Grandpa need to pack a bag and leave," he said, panic edging his voice. "The scanner app says the fire is almost to North Valley. Do you think we need to leave too?" Since I'd been in class for almost three hours, I didn't know what he meant, but I promised to figure out the danger level. I told him to sit tight and stay calm, even though I felt my own anxiety rising.

Thanks to social media and calls with friends, I realized Ben was excellent at listening to law enforcement scanners but less skilled at geography. The fire would probably not reach my parents' house, nor would it take out the town where we lived. Still, we could see flames on the Chehalem Mountains a few miles away, the night sky an eerie orange. We had friends on the hillside and knew their homes were in danger. A change in wind direction might also jeopardize our church at the city limits, which had become a staging area for farmers trying to evacuate livestock from their land on the mountain.

The world felt apocalyptic. Months earlier, the pandemic had ended my sons' high school careers. Their graduation was a drive-through affair. The looming threat of COVID-19 meant a summer of calculated risks for the boys, including whether saying goodbye to friends face-to-face might imperil their grandparents' lives. Now, Oregon was on fire, horses were stabled in the church parking lot, and we were all learning the language of fire perimeters and evacuation zones.

And we were the lucky ones.

I didn't know what to do. Calamity upon calamity kept affecting our community, so much so that my entry into parenting young adults was literally a trial by fire. There were no guidebooks I could consult that provided the insight I needed to help my sons and my students feel safe, not when COVID and forest fires, racial unrest, and a contentious political season seemed to threaten their early adulthood. Like many others just barely holding on to hope in a bleak pandemic year, I needed wisdom I didn't have and courage I couldn't muster to support the young people I love.

On that night in September, my husband was over two hundred miles away babysitting our grandchildren, and for the time being, I would have to muddle through these challenges alone. I downloaded a scanner app and listened for hours as firefighters worked to contain the rapidly spreading flames. When my son called after midnight, I was still awake, though I didn't know that the college had lost power, that students were huddled in dorm rooms, wondering how an already compromised school year might take one more turn for the worse.

My students were waiting in my nine o'clock class the next morning, having walked across campus through a miasma of smoke, the sky a dystopian gray. I could tell they were unsettled, bleary eyes peering out from mask-covered faces. They'd just been told to stay inside because of poor air quality, save for walking to classes. Another email from administrators reminded them not to congregate in groups indoors, because of COVID. Instead of comforting them that morning, I made a stupid joke about the rapture. And then apologized for the stupid joke, castigating myself for being so heartless. And then tried to teach a feature-writing class, my lesson on lead paragraphs seeming farcical when the world was ending.

I was flailing. We all were.

For the next ten days, students were sequestered in their dorm rooms, except for classes. The fire burned out, but the haze lingered, making everything about the school year even more complicated. When the sky finally cleared, when we could all breathe outside again, there would still be COVID restrictions, case counts, hybrid classes, risk calculations. That semester ended early to avoid having students carry germs back to campus post-Thanksgiving, and some of us had to celebrate the holidays without family because of the pandemic. By that point the United States was in another crisis, and many wondered whether then president Donald Trump would leave office peacefully come January. (Turns out the answer was no, in fact, he would not.)

In 2020, young adults faced a world unlike anything we'd ever experienced before. "Unprecedented times" became a common descriptor embraced by marketers and media, so much so that *unprecedented* was awarded word of the year for 2020, beating out *pandemic*, *COVID*, even *Zoom* as noun and verb. The phrase serves as a reminder that we are all out of our league, every last one of us. Those coming of age are trying to navigate run-of-the-mill young adult vagaries amid a global pandemic, with racial unrest and climate change, plus the threat of World War III, upending their lives. And those of us acting as mentors realize we don't have a clue what we're doing or how we can best support the young people we love as they transition to adulthood.

Most of us probably remember life after high school as a disruptive time, at least to some degree. The transition to adulthood caused upheaval in who we were, and in who we hoped to be. Now more than ever, though, every pathway to adulthood seems serpentine. The way forward is obstructed by barriers that folks in older generations may have constructed—like climate change, causing outsized natural disasters; a global pandemic that won't end; a growing national debt burden; and racial unrest sparked by white supremacy and fueled by social media. Those of us called to mentor young adults might be tempted to clear that pathway using tools that worked for us, but those tools are no longer adequate for the task we face. While the world burns during these *unprecedented times*, many of us are likewise undergoing mammoth transitions. Young people might be grappling with what happens next in their lives, but then so are we. How do any of us find our way into a settled future when the path feels so obscured? Can we really guide others when we feel lost? What do we do, really, when the children we love become young adults?

I have hope that there are answers to these questions, and that we can find our way forward together by seeking to understand the experiences of young adults, who see their generation's many challenges firsthand. My optimism is based on my quarter century as a teacher, meeting with countless students whose resilience and perseverance and faithfulness have made me a better person: more compassionate, more wise, more thoughtful. Their stories are the foundation of this book, and my conversations with former students have helped me understand better what is required of those who intend to shepherd young adults. My hope is also based on my experience parenting young adults who chose to forgo college and have manifest resolve in this decision, given that their father and mother are both lifelong educators. Being my sons' parent has been a gift, and the courage they've shown in pursuing their unique pathways has helped me be a more empathetic person, a stronger teacher, and a better friend.

I'm also someone who is still, always, trying to figure things out.

Here's one lesson I've learned: young adults are their own people, with their own agency. If you're like me, you may have tried to provide granular advice when the children you love reached young adulthood. If you're like me, you probably realized such advice isn't always welcomed. Parenting and working with young adults definitely helped me understand that any control I have over my children is illusory, and that they alone will decide their futures. Because young adults are autonomous beings, it's up to us to decide how we respond to who they are becoming, especially when our own expectations for them remain unfulfilled. Sure, we can provide input and resources, we can pray, we can hope the lessons we give them bear fruit in their lives. We can also choose ultimatums and intransigence, or the flexibility and grace and love that fosters healthy relationships. In other words, we can help them become who God created them to be in a world beset by chaos and crises no generation before has had to navigate.

Finding Our Way Forward is not a how-to book, nor can I provide ready advice about how to successfully guide young adults into a happily-ever-after life. Instead, I'd love you to see this book as an invitation, an opportunity to consider with me what it means to walk beside young people in unprecedented times, and what we can learn about ourselves on this journey. Along the way, I share stories from my experience and that of other older adults, as well as the insights of young people I know, who serve as expert witnesses to the culture forming them. We can consider together the unique pressures that young adults face today, as well as ways we might help them navigate the wild world we live in now. And we will explore how those pressures are shaping us and our relationships with the young people we love—our children, both literally and figuratively.

I hope this book will be useful not only for parents, but also for others who may have a different kind of relationship with young adults outside of family. Many people today have not only the family in which they grew up but also a found family, unrelated but coalesced around a shared appreciation and love for each other. Maybe there are young adults in your found family; maybe you work with young adults, or teach them, or mentor them. While this book might be primarily for parents, the insights offered here will help anybody who loves young adults.

Because I'm a writing teacher, and because I believe writing can be a powerful tool for processing our lived experience, the end of each chapter includes short exercises: queries designed to help you reflect on your understanding of young adults, and on the role you can take to help them find their way forward. Exercises like this are a defining part of most writing classes I teach, and while your work won't be graded,[1] I hope the questions might guide you in processing your specific contexts, and in clarifying the role you play in helping young adults become who God has created them to be. You might discover more about who you are created to be too.

As you read these pages, please note that when I use the term *young adult*, I generally mean people who have recently graduated from high school up until they turn twenty-five, the age at which the human brain is finally fully developed. At times, I may also mention Gen Z, the nomenclature describing people born between roughly 1997 and 2012. As I'm writing this book, the oldest of this generation are twenty-five, the youngest ten, and they've never lived in an era without the internet or cell phones, making them digital natives who don't even remember the thrilling buzz of a dial-up modem, let alone the crystal-clear sound of audio cassette tapes playing on a two-deck boom box.

Writing from a Christian perspective is tricky, too, given the many iterations of Christian faith in the United States, let alone the world. Though it's tempting to argue that my brand of Anabaptism is the One True Faith, and to assert that all other expressions of Christianity are lacking, I recognize this is simply not true. Still, I use Christians as a shorthand for people with a commonly held set of beliefs centered on the life and teachings of Jesus. At points, I identify white evangelicals specifically, simply because they have had an outsized influence in US politics and cultural conversations, and because of their profoundly negative impact on many young Christians.

Finally, I changed some names in this book to protect the identity of people willing to share their perspectives: as parents, teachers, and pastors who helped raise young adults, as well as those now in the throes of young adulthood. Even though their names may be fictitious, the people are real, and I'm grateful for their willingness to tell their stories. Interviewing so many amazing people has been transformative for me, and I'm thankful for their time, often shared over lattes from the best coffee shop in my hometown. There are few greater pleasures in life than drinking chai lattes with young adults whose goodness in unprecedented times sustains me, helping me find my way when I feel lost.

The prophet Micah lived during unprecedented times as well, and knew firsthand what it meant to face a world on fire, the evils of corrupted power and injustice afflicting Israel. Micah 6:8 outlines how people should respond when facing a world on fire. What were his listeners called to do when challenged by inequities? Micah says that God "has shown you . . . what is good. And what does the LORD require of you? To act justly and to love mercy and to walk humbly with your God."

I am drawn to the seeming simplicity of this prescription, three clear, compelling steps God wants us to take. *Finding Our Way Forward* is informed by the wisdom of this Micah passage and shaped by Jesus' insistence that the greatest commandment resides not in legalism and piety, but in extending love to God, and mercy to our neighbors. These directives are so straightforward, and while we can have countless quibbles over what Scripture says about a number of theological issues, the Bible is clear about what God calls us to. Do justice. Love mercy. Walk humbly. In other words, Love God. Love your neighbors.

In the challenging moments of my work with young adults, when I don't know how to reassure my sons because our state is on fire; or when I make misguided jokes about the rapture to calm a classroom; or when I can't offer hope to beleaguered students because I am also despairing: when I'm struggling to make sense of a world I don't understand, I'm reminded of who God calls me to be. Not an expert providing conclusive wisdom about the world to pass on to later generations. The work to which I'm really called is similar to what is required of us all: to do justice, love kindness, walk humbly, love others, and love God. These callings are tempered by God's unending grace, which catches me again and again when I fail.

We're walking in unfamiliar territory, all of us. We're navigating a pandemic and climate crises and the threat of war and political extremism and untold barriers that impede our flourishing. Yet when we feel lost, there is wisdom to guide us, and God's holy voice, calling us all to respond. This book is an attempt to understand how we can face unprecedented times with the young adults we love, and how we can find our way forward together.

ONE

With a Grateful Heart

became a stepparent on the edge of a sludgy pond, and a first-time mother in a taxicab, hurtling through Saigon traffic. Both events happened in September, five years apart, a knitting together of a new family that to this day stuns me by its goodness and its complexity, in equal measure. To know me is to know this story: of how two sets of kids, separated by two decades (and none born to me), became family, a miracle that continues to unfurl, even today, as my sons enter adulthood.

When I married my husband by the mighty shores of Tilikum Lake in 1997, I acquired his beloved red Jeep Cherokee, a farmhouse I quickly learned to despise, his sagging furniture, and his two children, who were then seventeen and thirteen. Of the lot, it's obviously the stepchildren I'm most grateful for, and while the jeep, the house, and the furniture all eventually disappeared from our lives, my connection to Melissa and Ryan has deepened, thanks in great part to their dad's persisting admiration of and fidelity to them, as well as their expansive love for their brothers, who are decades younger.

Back when we first married, when Ron and I would huddle together on our dilapidated couch in our dilapidated house, I vaguely understood my relationship to Melissa and Ryan could be a challenge. I'd arrived on the scene seven years after my husband's divorce, so I wasn't an interloper by any stretch, but I knew the trope of devious stepmother in *Cinderella* and *Snow White*. And while I didn't consider myself wicked, I was only twelve years older than my stepdaughter, more peer than parent. Besides, they already had a loving mother who lived five miles away from us, where they spent much of their time. We were the every-other-weekend family, the home away from home. My husband delighted in the time he had with his kids, and because he delighted, I did too.

We definitely were not the family engaged in the day-to-day challenges of shepherding mercurial teenagers into adulthood. That role primarily went to their mom, and so we often stood on the sidelines, serving as cheerleaders to Melissa's and Ryan's decisions, and also (pardon the mixed metaphor) as backup, ready to step into the game, to offer advice and encouragement when called.

By the time Ron and I married, I was nearing thirty. Most of my friends had weddings right after college and were one or two babies into motherhood. My twenties had been spent wrestling with anger at God, who as far as I could tell wasn't answering any of my prayers about finding a mate. People joyfully talked about God's blessing of a partner and my insides would cave; I wondered what was wrong with me, and why God hadn't similarly blessed me. Was I too ugly? Too opinionated? Too much to be loved? One sibling got married, and then the other a month later, and I was still alone, third-wheeling my way through family and church functions, wondering whether I would ever find a spouse. Finally, I met Ron through a mutual friend, and we began a long-distance correspondence. I couldn't believe my luck, God's providence manifest in a nearly immediate connection I'd never know before.

Because of a decade-long struggle with singleness, I often hesitate to express this providence in a way that acknowledges those young people who long for marriage and family and are left wanting. Who pray as earnestly as I did, and who find their prayers unanswered in ways that would give them a similar largesse: a loving spouse, the children they hope to raise. Is it possible to understand gratitude, and to convey the necessity of a grateful heart, to young adults who might be stuck in circumstances not of their own making, anger roiling to a God who seems silent in the face of earnest prayer?

This is a question with which I still wrestle, decades removed from experiencing this silence, from feeling utter despair, and while in another challenging season, when my sons are trying to find their own way to settled adulthood. Like so many other people their age, Ben and Sam are fighting against an onslaught of messages reminding them that God's providence is reflected in a narrowly circumscribed understanding of success for people their age: admission to college, the beginnings of a lucrative career, self-sufficiency. And of course, finding true love, preparing for a family, delighting in the accoutrements of independence, like a nice car and a good cell phone plan.

If the children you love don't follow the typical path into adulthood, you might also sometimes wonder whether you can express gratitude in the face of significant challenges. Parents whose children are struggling to find purchase into adulthood might look on other parents with gut-wrenching envy, wondering where their own lives went off course. Sometimes, rejoicing can be exceedingly difficult when one's own child appears aimless while other young people are receiving lucrative scholarships, making a seamless transition to college, forming fast friendships with dormmates, and landing prestigious internships. Social media posts celebrating these joyful moments with the hashtag #blessed might raise the same kind of questions I had when, in my twenties, I wondered why God was not blessing me. We may consider whether we can possibly express gratitude when the young adults we love don't have the normal markings of a #blessed life.

And what about those young adults who forgo college, work a series of low-paying jobs, and need to live in their parents' bonus room? The ones who cast about through their twenties, looking for vocational opportunities? Who face their twenty-fifth birthday without a partner or a close community? To be honest, most of us would not say that this path reflects God's profligacy, though we rarely ask ourselves why we've decided to make thanksgiving conditional, especially when the Gospels remind us, again and again, that *not as the world gives do I give to you* (John 14:27 ESV).

Expressing gratitude might require that we believe what Jesus tells us, and act accordingly, not in changing young adults' conditions, but in changing the narratives that outline what it means to know God's blessing at this age. Those narratives need revision, at any rate, especially the scripts demanding that high-school graduates run straight to college, that Christian college graduates have a degree and a ring by spring, that twentysomethings be in the first steps of a lucrative career. If we could write new narratives, we might see that providence extends beyond our simple definitions of what life should look like. Because until we believe that each young adult is a unique expression of God's favor, it will be difficult to look on some young people's lives—and our own—and deeply believe that those lives are worthy of thanksgiving.

Hired as an adjunct instructor for two classes of first-year composition, I began teaching at George Fox University the month I married Ron. While working as an adjunct, I finished my doctoral comprehensive exams, then my dissertation, grateful that Ron's full-time salary could support my efforts. Melissa matriculated at George Fox the same year I started teaching, and hours before the wedding, was approached by peers who expressed wonder and awe that their cool, young writing teacher was marrying her dad. Did she know? Was she aware?

A secret wedding would be a twist in the wicked stepmother story line, but no, Melissa played a role in the ceremony, and both kids signed our marriage certificate. We were officially a family then, though I had no real understanding of what that meant, nor how I should relate to two teenagers now my own, nor to the students whom I'd encounter back in class the following Monday, four weeks into my vocation as a Christian university professor.

Five years later, we decided to expand our family through adoption. By that point, we'd moved into town, a mouse infestation having scared me away from the crumbling farm-house for good. Melissa had graduated from college, Ryan from high school. My husband, who loved being a father, was game for another round of child-rearing. And so, in September 2002, we adopted Benjamin Quan, a seven-month-old from Vietnam, taking a week off from teaching to meet Benjamin in a small but brightly lit orphanage near Saigon. On the morning we first held him in Bien Hoa, I felt more caregiver than parent, cradling this unfamiliar baby wearing a blue and red jumper.

Finally, the paperwork signed, Benjamin was handed to us through the passenger door of a Saigon taxi, which delivered us to our hotel. He weighed only twelve pounds, with wispy hair and limbs, and was breathtakingly beautiful. Benjamin had fallen asleep in my arms as we weaved through traffic congested by cyclos and honking cars. At the hotel, I put him on our king-size bed, and Ron and I stretched out on either side of this tiny child, watching him sleep for the next few hours. I couldn't believe I'd become a parent and didn't know what to do next.

For twenty years, I've sustained that wonder: How did I get to be a parent to this person, and to his brother, Samuel Saurabh, whom we adopted from India three years later? How did I get to be a stepparent to two extraordinary adults, and a grandparent to two boys? And also, at every parenting stage I wonder:

What in the heck are we supposed to do next?

Somehow, in some way, we have muddled through. At times, I feel like my younger self watching my sleeping infant in Vietnam, an observer to the wonderful gift at my life's center; at times, I wonder whether I will ever figure out this parenting gig, or even how to relate (imperfectly or not) with the young people who inhabit my world. Most of the time, I'm astounded by God's providence in creating my family, aware as well that my bounty is predicated on loss: my sons' loss of their birth families and culture; my stepchildren's loss of their first family; my husband's loss of time with his older children, a fractured marriage still complicating his holidays and the visits we are afforded with grandchildren.

Still, on the rare occasions now when we can all be together, my house made full by family unified through circumstance or providence or the lucky alignment of all the right stars, I recognize how fortunate I am, a recipient of so much good. Thanksgiving comes easily in those moments, and after a weekend with family, when the entire hallway is choked by random shoes and toys and books, and my own big kids are sleeping on the couch because their nephews have taken their beds, and the kitchen is buzzing with requests for snacks, I breathe deeply into the gratitude that this gets to be my life.

This is an extravagance I could not have anticipated when, as a young adult, I felt an ache of loneliness so deep, it turned me for a stretch against God. And I also wonder, what if the emptiness had persisted? If Ron and his kids and our kids hadn't found each other? Even then, God would call me to gratitude—and I hope, even then, I would have answered.

Three years after getting married, and just as I finished my dissertation, a position in my discipline opened at George Fox, and after a nationwide search, the faculty decided I would be just fine for the role, another undeserving gift for which I hope my work serves as thanksgiving. I awake most days eager to spend time talking to young people whose brilliance has ignited my passion to teach for several decades. Being a professor is a life better than anything I could imagine when I was in college deliberating about my future. Like many of my students, I spent four years as an undergraduate casting about for direction, and when I finally found it long after graduation, I still wasn't sure the life of the mind was for me. Yet here I am, years into my tenure as a writing instructor, delighted by the work to which I've been called.

My sons' growth has been measured not in the ticked marks on a doorframe at home, but in the rhythms of an academic calendar. We have lived by those rhythms of the school year their entire upbringing, and the boys know that their dad will be grading essays on Christmas Eve, their mom creating fall syllabi around the Fourth of July. Benjamin and Samuel grew up on campus, as babies sleeping and playing under my desk and as preschoolers running across the quad. They went to women's basketball games with us, climbing the bleachers while we cheered on the Bruins' dominant teams. The boys sat in our classes when we had school and they didn't, and ate lunch at the cafe alongside faculty colleagues, including one communications teacher they called Santa. Still today, cafeteria workers and administrative assistants and colleagues ask after them by name: *How are Ben-and-Sam?*—just the one name a signifier for two.

Each year, the boys got closer and closer to my students' ages, becoming peers rather than cute little kids who drew on chalkboards and drank hot cocoa with their mom. Conversations with my husband about the kids attending George Fox seemed theoretical, a hazy future we would one day reach, but not now. Then now arrived, and both my kids decided against attending the campus where they'd grown up, the one where they could each receive a free education through tuition remission. Despite their parents' vocations, Ben-and-Sam had other plans for their lives, ones that didn't necessarily include college, at least not yet. Sam came to that conclusion before high school had even ended; Ben, after one year at George Fox, where he found a serious girlfriend, a longing for service, and a realization that the academic life might not be for him.

When I go to work, I see my sons' faces in the students I teach. They are the same age now, navigating the same challenges, though in entirely different contexts. Both boys have expanded my empathy for my students; and the students I teach have deepened my respect for my sons, a synergy I never anticipated when Ben-and-Sam were playing LEGO on my office floor. Soon, those who sit in my classes will be younger than my kids, and I will be more grandma than mother to the young people who drop by my office, looking for someone to listen, to placate their homesickness, to remind them that their stories matter too. For now, these minutes between classes, when I connect with a student who connects with me: this also is good, an expression of love for which I am grateful.

The past few years have not been without their difficulties. Like a multitude of other young people their age, both Ben and Sam have struggled, trying to find their way forward with a million and more competing voices telling them who and what they should be. As young men of color, they have contended with explicit racism and implicit biases. Adopted into a white family, Ben and Sam uniquely navigate questions about their identities, and I haven't always known how best to help them. We've gone through long periods when we are all wearied by late nights and tears, when I've stretched myself out on the floor, begging God to show me how I can be a better parent to my boys.

In these moments, I remind myself that no matter what happens, each day as a mother to Ben and Sam has been a gift for which I am grateful. That even the challenges we face are a chance to develop a deeper store of empathy for others who are likewise struggling: parents overwhelmed by the hard work of trying to figure out their own children; and young adults, surviving in a world that seems especially hostile right now.

This life, my life, has been a miracle, for which my every breath should express thanksgiving, because even that breath is a gift, given by a profligate God who created each of us and called us each good. Frederick Buechner describes this gift as "the grace of God," the world transformed by our mere presence in it. "The grace of God means something like [this]," he writes in *Listening to Your Life*. "Here is your life. You might never have been, but you are because the party wouldn't have been complete without you. Here is the world. Beautiful and terrible things will happen. Don't be afraid. I am with you. Nothing can ever separate us. It's for you I created the universe."[1] Imagine believing that our individuality is so great that the world wouldn't be the same without us. That our unique journeys, as young adults and as the people who love them, are worthy of a universe's creation. That God is with us no matter the direction we take. It seems like this alone would be grounds for gratitude.

Teaching gives me unique access to the grace of God, which is manifested in my students' life stories. In most classes, I remind my students of the interplay between our individual lives and universal understanding, and that writing powerfully knits together the individual and universal, allowing us to connect with strangers across an expanse of space and time, as well as classmates squeezed into uncomfortable desks right there, in the same room. Even though my students often write about similar experiences, I see a blessed individuality threaded into the words they choose. A few years ago, I had the phrase *fearfully, wonderfully made* tattooed on my arm, an echo of Psalm 139:14: "I praise you because I am fearfully and wonderfully made." It is a reminder to me of my worth and also, I hope, a reminder to others—that God made them wonderfully and is astounded by that creation.

This grace of God does not mean we are saved from suffering and sadness, nor can we protect the young adults we love from the suffering that will surely be part of their experience as humans. My own significant privilege has shielded me from some of this suffering, more so than many of my students, more so than my own children. And still, despite my family's relative privilege, we have struggled. At times, I long for the exuberant closeness I see in other families, at least on social media. My sons' unique stories have included heartache because of their adoptions, because of their skin color, because of learning challenges that made school much harder than it was for many of their peers. In other ways, they are lucky: their parents are still happily married, for one. We also have financial resources that mean we don't worry each month about making ends meet, nor have my kids faced significant illness or disability, all factors that can complicate a person's journey to adulthood. When we talk about finding our way with young adults, I need to acknowledge that for some people, that road forward is compromised by obstacles that can make the journey far more difficult than it has been for me and (at least in some ways) for mine.

Having said that, I also want to proclaim that each life, including my own, is in its own way a miracle. Even if it were all wiped away tomorrow, I hope I would still be grateful for the twenty-five years I've been married, the twenty-two years I've been a professor, the twenty years I've been a mother, the year I've been an empty nester trying to establish a life without my sons at home. Being grateful means recognizing that each moment is a gift, no matter whether you are a young adult trying to find your way forward or someone who has accrued many more years, and so many more gifts, God's prolificacy written into your life story. That story itself is testament to your fearful, wonderful creation, to the beauty of your unique journey.

At a retreat several years ago, I was lamenting to a woman in her eighties about my sons growing up, about time passing so quickly, about being solidly middle-aged. Her grandchildren were my sons' age, one of them a favorite student in my classes at George Fox. Tearing up, she said, "I said the same thing when I was your age: it all goes so fast." The comment reminded me that this journey is fleeting, and in no time I will be much nearer to my life's end—though, of course, we never fully know the place or time when death will take us. Even at the end, though, I want to be grateful for the chance this life has given me, to be a college professor whose twenty-year-old sons have chosen not to attend college—at least not yet. An English instructor and writer whose children hated reading. A deeply committed pacifist whose child is serving in the military. An elder in the Quaker church who understands why young people are leaving organized religion.

A stepmother who is neither wicked nor villainous, and a grandmother who feels too young for that role.

And finally, I want to be grateful as an image bearer of God, whose unending grace sustains me. I know that this grace, more than anything else, is good.

Three days before Christmas in 2021, I was exhausted. After a challenging few months at work, I craved some time to myself, with only a book or Netflix to keep me company. But when the adults in your family have work and school schedules to keep and only a small window of time to celebrate the holidays, you accommodate their schedules, rather than your own.

My sons had arrived on different flights the night before, and we drove home from the airport through the empty midnight streets, giddy they had arrived, even if way past my bedtime. The semester had concluded days earlier, hours before my stepdaughter Melissa and her family drove down from Seattle. Benjamin's fiancé was due on our doorstep at any moment, and the house was humming. I still had some shopping to do, and gift wrapping, and meal planning, play-acting the stereotypical harried mom of every holiday special, no doubt in need of an ethereal lesson about the True Meaning of Christmas.

What better way to amp up the chaos, and my weariness, than with our first annual gingerbread competition? I'm not sure who had the idea for a *Great British Bake Off*/*Nailed It!* mash-up, Mock family style, but Melissa gathered up all the ingredients, we strategically set up teams of three people each, and at the designated time, we went to work on our creations. My team clearly had creative and intellectual geniuses, with my ten-year-old grandson Enzo and my son-in-law Rahul immediately building a structurally unsound gingerbread house, its collapse making the three of us laugh into tears.

Ryan was the only family member not at our competition, and when our creations were finished he called by video to serve as impartial judge. He gave each team an award, honoring our efforts, though I think the overall winner had reconstructed the Alamo, a nod to Benjamin's then home at a naval base in San Antonio. The ninety minutes we spent in this new holiday tradition, making space for every family member's contribution, became for me the highlight of our time together, all of us drawn from different parts of the States for a few moments of laughter, and a very messy kitchen. Whatever exhaustion I felt had vanished in pure joy, for me and my husband, for my sons and grandsons, for our entire family, together for a rare moment in an otherwise busy and isolated pandemic year.

Those flashes of joy can seem few and far between, especially in a time when everything feels wrong about the world, with division and chaos and death separating families and communities and making us all bowed under the weight of so much sorrow. Finding our way with the young adults we love means thanksgiving for even these most banal moments, praising God for the pure joy found in the fleeting hours before Christmas, when a kitchen smeared with frosting and gingerbread dust feels magical.

SHORT EXERCISES

1. Consider the story of your family's becoming. How does that unique story reflect God's providence, bearing witness to God's goodness in your life?

2. Where have you experienced challenges in your relationship with the young adults in your life? In what ways could those challenges also be a call to gratitude?

3. Write a letter to the young adults in your life, reflecting on the ways they are fearfully, wonderfully made (Psalm 139:14) and also expressing thanksgiving for the extravagant gift of their lives in the world.

TWO

To Discovering Your Calling(s)

God bless well-meaning strangers and grandparents alike, those who earnestly want to relate to young adults and ask the question that comes first to their minds: *What's next for you?* Inquisitors are well-intentioned when they wonder where young adults will go to college (as if college is predetermined for all), what they will study, what career deserves their lifetime commitment. We assume every eighteen-year-old knows with full assurance exactly what this will be, and we may have little awareness that our questions, often spun out into empty space, heap shame on the heads of young people who haven't a clue about what's next.

God bless every single person who misuses the words of poets, who quotes Mary Oliver or Robert Frost, who wonders about precious lives or the road less traveled. Lord knows that includes me, a teacher of English, who dragged Oliver's poem "The Summer Day" into my first-year classes, asked my students to answer the inexorable question about what they plan to do before they die, how they will spend the fleeting minutes of their too-short lives. Does an eighteen-year-old, weeks into college, need to answer this question? Can she make significant rest-of-life choices this early into adulthood?

So most of all, God bless the young adults, those who respond with politeness to each inquiry, even when they'd rather take a vow of silence than answer one more time the ubiquitous question: *What's next for you?* God bless those who describe elaborate plans for a future they can't fully imagine, whether to be kind or to save face or because they believe everyone else (save them) knows with complete confidence what's next. No doubt they feel wholly alone in their unknowing. God bless them all in their angst and discomfort, for the uncertain are more common than they realize.

God bless them, and their fumbling answers to questions about what they will do. May we honor them anyway, finding our way forward together no matter the roads they travel, and no matter the roads we've taken too.

I don't remember much about my lurching journey after high school graduation. I took the SATs because my parents told me I should, then applied to a few colleges, choosing one because of an athletic scholarship and not much else. Even back then, well-meaning friends and family asked about my next steps, where I'd be going to college, which seemed the only possible choice for a white, lower-middle-class child of college graduates. The drumbeat about calling and vocation didn't sound so loudly then as it does for young people now, though in my final semester at college, those "What's next?" questions started to take on real heft, and I scrambled to figure out an answer. I signed on for a year of Mennonite voluntary service, thinking God might be calling me to the inner city, which seemed the most likely place—other than overseas mission work—where God would want me. Perhaps I'd heard my calling wrongly, though, because the ministry I landed on definitely wasn't in my skill set; I cried after work most days, aware that my privileged white-girl-savior intentions couldn't alleviate the suffering of people who were poor and elderly and alone. After my year of service ended, I spent the next sixth months living in my parents' basement and working retail at a nearby mall. This wasn't my calling either, I realized as I miserably hounded customers into buying suits, knowing nothing about matching sports coats and ties.

What's next? Certainly not *that*.

Finally, I landed on graduate school as a shrug to the universe, to the very idea of vocation. Might as well get my master's degree in English, I thought, which seemed as good a choice as any, since I could delay career decisions for a few more years while I studied, and I wouldn't have to continue upselling men with a pocket square that potentially matched the tie. Teaching English seemed like a cool idea, but I hadn't sensed the Holy Spirit calling me to that career. There were no nighttime visitations from Jesus affirming my decision. No doors magically opening to make the pathway clear. No real encouragement from the adults in my life to take one path or the other. I wanted someone to tell me what to do—give me a five-point plan to my future, even—and all I heard was nothing, a resounding silence.

So graduate school it was. The path of least resistance. Ironic, I know. Few people would perceive graduate school as the *easiest* route to adulthood, what with the stressors of intense studies coupled with little to no income, yet some young people choose more schooling—college, graduate school, or law school—because they don't know what else to do. When you've been a student for most of your life, choosing more school can seem like the most comfortable option, the best way to spend your time. Or at least the next few years.

My route to adulthood was definitely circuitous, and your own pathway to adulthood no doubt included stops and starts, redirections, ill-informed decisions to change purpose, choices distilled through a white-hot process of anxiety and second-guessing. This is normal, despite the persistent efforts we make to help young adults choose a calling. Over half of Americans change their jobs every one to five years, and the average worker has at least twelve different roles during their lifetime. Of those who attend college, anywhere from 30 percent to 80 percent change their majors at least once; the data on this is imprecise, and doesn't necessarily capture those who stick with a major or a career they dislike. According to one study, 61 percent of college graduates reported wishing they'd chosen a different major.[1]

Because we know that finding a vocation is fluid, and that people make determinations about careers throughout their lifespan, why do we still insist that young adults need to decide now how their entire future will be spent? The persistence of "What's next?" inquiries creates unmitigated stress in young people's lives, as well as paralyzing anxiety. Believing that career decisions at eighteen or twenty-one or twenty-five will shape an entire future makes any choice fraught, especially when that choice seems to inform future happiness and the accoutrements of the good life. Hearing that God is calling them can stoke even more angst, though it's offered as a hopeful declaration: God has a plan for you!

When God's call is only an imperceptible whisper, or when prayers about guidance are met with silence, it's hard to know to what God is calling us. If we insist on asking young people *How do you plan to spend your life?*, we also should hold space for this honest answer: *I don't know.*

The same year I started graduate school, I also began my career, teaching two sections of first-year composition alongside my studies. In English programs, graduate students often teach introductory classes in exchange for funding, and the gig seemed like a good deal, though I was paid a pittance for the hours I spent grading essays and planning classes. At the time, this seemed like a boon—a clear sign that God had called me to this work, even though I had zero training and no idea how to teach. Decades later, I recognize the exploitative system that uses graduate students as cheap academic labor.

Two weeks before my first class and for my twenty-fourth birthday, my parents gave me a black attaché case nearly identical to one owned by an undergraduate professor I idolized. I'd described the case in intricate detail on my birthday wish list, no doubt hoping a professor's good teaching mojo might be portable in a sixty-dollar leather product my parents bought at Sears. Carrying my new case, I immediately felt older, more accomplished. It didn't occur to me that the shiny unblemished leather might have given away the game. I was clearly a novice.

I'd had one whole week of training on how to teach writing courses when I stepped into my first class, and even ten times that amount didn't seem like enough. My students, only a few years younger than me, could see in my shaking hands that the person standing before them was scared to death. Since these were all first-year students, it could be that they were also pretending, conveying confidence none of us felt. That classroom in Lucas Hall was thick with anxiety.

Arriving too early to class that morning was my first mistake. Or maybe my first was wearing paisley culottes with a sleeveless, orange mock turtleneck, and arriving too early was my second. I set out my syllabi and textbooks on the lectern, then paced back and forth by the chalkboard, much like a caged animal anxiously seeking an exit. As students filtered in, I walked out, found a drinking fountain, took deep gulps of water, then wandered back inside. More students arrived. The clock ticked minutes slowly, until it was finally time.

I started talking, choking back tears, my voice wavering. Something about assignments, I said. And taking roll. And how I wanted to help them learn to write well, but that they would need to work hard too. My tearful voice steadied, but I don't remember whether that first class even lasted the entire fifty minutes, since I really didn't have much to say. I imagine the students left the room shaking their heads, wondering about the holy mess they'd just witnessed. The attaché case, at least, was spectacular.

After several decades, I'm a better teacher, thanks be to God, shaped not so much by the wisdom of pedagogical theory as by the challenges of each semester; and the experience to know what assignments work, and what fails spectacularly; and the courage to try new technology on occasion, even when a dittoed handout and overhead projector might work just as well. More than that, though, being a writing instructor and interacting with young people has helped me become more empathetic, more sincere, more thoughtful, more rooted in my faith.

It might be easy to conclude that my vocation alone has made me a better person, reflective of God's blessing on me for choosing rightly. Some might believe that happily staying in the same job at the same university for twenty years reflects the synergy Frederick Buechner describes—where *the world's deepest longings, my deepest joy* happily meet.[2] Most Christian discussions suggest as much about vocation: that when we fulfill God's calling, we find delight and a deeper, more fulfilling sense of ourselves, of others, of God. Yet I often contemplate a more complicated understanding. It's not one call that has made me become more who God created me to be, but the multitude of callings to which I have committed my life, to following the teachings of Jesus and all that following entails. Those who answer these other calls, the Gospels say, are the ones who will truly be blessed. So why this intent focus on career, rather than the many other ways we are called by God?

The language of *calling* is often used as a cudgel and a carrot for young adults, whether they attend college or go right into the workforce. In Christian environments especially, God's calling has specific application, at least where vocation is concerned. We ask high school graduates whether they are called to attend college, or whether a gap year calling might include mission work. We use the impetus of God's calling to help those who matriculate in picking a major and deciding on classes. As commencement approaches, we ask students where they are called to next, and whether that calling will include more schooling, matrimony, or a job in their chosen field of study. The language of calling is woven into my institution's mission statement, in a way that one young adult described as "very aggressive." Because I know well the ethos of Christian higher education, I'm pretty sure other schools aggressively use calling in their mission statements, too, and define calling narrowly as a signifier for "a godly career."

For many Christians, the idea of God's calling is intertwined primarily with notions of work. Hannah W., twenty-five, described this understanding well, having attended two Christian institutions and now working at one: "The evangelical idea of calling means that a person has one skill set that they are obliged to use in a ministerial way that also produces capital. It leads to the idea that a person can only have 'one' of these." In this, she echoed the theory of the German philosopher Max Weber, who argued that the marriage of calling with vocation reflects a capitalistic impulse. Weber traced through the history of Western culture a pressing need to compel people to work mundane jobs that bring little personal satisfaction. Christian capitalists could endow jobs with a sense of purpose by suggesting that God calls people to those roles. Weber used the example of a cobbler who does the repetitive work of making shoes every day. If one is called to produce shoes, what seems a mundane task becomes an endeavor blessed by God.

In this vein, those truly answering God's call, using the skill set God has given them, don't need to be paid a just wage. This reasoning is probably why, as a pastor's daughter, I had to wear clothes from Goodwill and eat free school lunches. The congregation had told my dad that because his call was in service to God, his salary need not be extravagant, or even substantive enough for his family to thrive. In a conversation on Twitter, several people who have worked in Christian institutions noted that this same impulse made it easier for their workplace to use the idea of calling to manipulate employees, often implicitly, sometimes explicitly. If believers are doing God's calling, the thinking goes, their pay and benefits need not be as significant; if they are called to work forty hours a week for Jesus, working sixty hours a week might be okay too.

Young adults have internalized these problematic messages about vocation and respond to queries about calling with a good bit of cynicism, recognizing the marriage of calling and capitalism as the antithesis to what they read in Scripture. They characterize conversations about calling as manipulative, as "detrimental foisting" on them of adults' perspectives about career, which according to Colin, twenty-four, "sows confusion and doubt, leading a person to do what they should not do." For Hannah J., twenty-seven, this kind of language around calling "sucks the joy out of doing something for fun if you feel obligated to perform it as your so-called vocation."

Another young adult, Jen, saw the drumbeat of this language around vocation as "selfish," and believed that the inordinate focus on calling for people her age simply became a "cheap excuse" for someone to do what they wanted to do anyway. Saying God was calling them to one job or another provided easy justification for their own wish fulfillment, whether they were skilled in that role or not. One person admitted that they "can't get past the feeling that no one is really 'calling' [people]; they're just responding to an impulse they feel strongly about, and pointing it to God."

In the year my sons were both eighteen and preparing for next steps in their lives, I started to recognize how ubiquitous the language of calling can be, and why it feels so aggressive. The idea of vocation was presented to them everywhere, from the college admissions counselors they met to the military recruiters trying to convince my son that God might be calling him to the armed forces. Because I'd also internalized messages about vocation, I simply reinforced the sense that my kids needed to figure out what career they wanted to pursue and get to it: even though, in middle age, I still sometimes question whether I've been doing the work to which I've been called.

When Benjamin and Samuel graduated from high school, long conversations about what they hoped for after graduation were often met with an exasperated cry (sometimes literally). "How should I know?" each one of my sons said at one point or another. "I'm only eighteen." Many times, our discussions stretched long into the night, as one or the other son—and sometimes both—expressed a lack of clarity about what they should be doing next. I was unprepared for the intensity of these talks, for the despair my kids felt, even though I'd believed we weren't pressuring them, weren't making them go to college or compelling them to have a specific, detailed plan in place post-graduation. As badly as I wanted them to pick a lane, giving me a degree of comfort, they were exactly right. What did they know about the world, really, after being in the same hometown for their entire lives? We were asking them to make a choice about their futures, and they didn't even know the options available to them yet.

At one time, the first-year curriculum at my institution included a class intended to help students explore God's calling. I loved teaching the fresh-eyed young people, not yet jaded by the pressures of college, still awed by cafeteria food and the independence of dorm life. Discussions focused, in part, on hearing God's call, inventorying personal strengths and applying them to that place Frederick Buechner describes as "where your deep gladness and the world's deep hunger meet."[3] About two months into the semester, a young woman took that message to heart, realizing she wasn't called to be in college. She left for beauty school; she loved applying makeup and doing hair. Yet the course had been created for retention, with a goal of keeping students at our institution for all four years. It seemed as if I'd failed in this instance, especially since becoming a makeup artist didn't match the high-minded callings we were talking about in class, those for which an expensive four-year degree is required.

I wonder whether the course outcomes reflected an aggressive approach to vocation, and whether the idea that eighteen-year-olds should seek God's calling is entangled with expectations about success. After all, our culture insists that success for young adults looks like a clear plan for the future, a well-paying job, and independent living—a vision of success that has, ironically, created a student debt crisis whereby countless young people take out hefty college loans to fund the degrees they presumably need to unlock doors to a good life to which God calls them. Could being a beautician really advance God's kingdom? The answer is yes, absolutely. The course had worked, though not necessarily as we'd intended. The young woman realized that God's call didn't include university, at least not then, and she stepped aside to pursue another calling, a worthy endeavor, though different from what our university had anticipated.

The countless jokes deriding people who live in their parents' basement reflects our communal discomfort with young people who don't find immediate independence after high school. The shrinking interest in some college majors points to this impulse as well, with parents pushing their children into more lucrative fields like engineering, nursing, and business. Increasingly, young people are being steered away from the humanities, and I've had numerous conversations with skeptical parents on college visits about why being an English major opens up vocational possibilities, noting that if their children really don't want to pursue a business degree, maybe it's for the best that they feel free to explore their options.

Insisting that young adults prepare for specific vocations reflects the capitalistic—and specifically, the classist—nature of our discussions around calling. Because when we talk about a Christian calling, we are primarily focused on professional work for which higher education is a necessity, rather than seeing other types of careers as those to which our young adults might be called. We are unlikely to claim that someone who works a fast-food drive-up window is called to that position, or that a person who works at a winery pruning vines six days a week has heard God's call and responded. My younger son's journey after high school has helped me see most clearly the classist nature of my ideas about calling. Sam works in a restaurant, enjoys his colleagues, and wants to move up in the industry. For a long while, his dad and I thought he'd be a great teacher and coach, and we talked about how he needed to "catch the vision of his calling." Truly believing the idea of God's call, though, means accepting that

Samuel might be called as a server, or a bartender, or a restaurant manager, and that this calling, far different from what I've imagined for Sam, is more than enough.

Wanting young people to seek God's calling should compel us to support their pursuits and give them opportunities to experience different pathways—even if they decide that being a history major, or not attending college at all, or being a host for a chain restaurant is what they are called to do. My conversations with young adults and their general cynicism about the language of vocation suggest that we need to reevaluate whether we are manipulative in our use of vocation and calling, and whether we have a limited imagination about God. We might want to ask what assumptions we make when we provide young people advice about God's call. If we've decided that some callings are more acceptable than others—that being an engineer is somehow more righteous than waiting tables, or a nursing major more worthy of our resources than someone studying English—it could be that we've missed the mark.

But it could also be that our application of the word *calling* is all wrong, and that we have at best an incomplete understanding of what it means to be called by God and to be faithful to this calling.

Here's the thing:

My calling was not fulfilled once I signed a tenure-track contract in 2000, even though I talk about being called to teach at George Fox as if it were a one-and-done proposition. The language we use around calling not only betrays our sense that God's calling is vocational, but also suggests that once we understand what God wants us to do vocationally—once we find "our calling"—we can settle in and enjoy the work forever and evermore. Emma, twenty-two, felt this pressure acutely when she was an undergraduate trying to land on her calling. "I felt like *I* had to figure out the exact thing God wanted for me, rather than just seeking to express my identity in him naturally as I went about my life," she said. The institutional apparatus around her to support this search was of little use because it was up to Emma to hear the Holy Spirit calling her to a specific vocation, and it was up to her to respond to that specificity.

This is one reason I've questioned my call to teach from the very first time I pulled on my paisley culottes and stepped into the classroom, pretty much alone in my determination of what I should do with my life. As a young teacher, I looked for signs everywhere that I was doing God's bidding, wondering whether a job opening at George Fox in my discipline constituted a sign of faithfulness to God's calling, questioning whether I was really using the gifts God had given me. I worried I'd missed my calling entirely because I didn't have a momentous breakthrough when doors opened or slammed shut, the big hand of God pointing out the vocational path I should take. Instead, indecision and confusion and questions have persisted throughout my life as I have waited for the Spirit to call me. What I've received in return is mostly God's silence, not the resounding Voice of God I've been told would direct my path.

That our calling is supposed to reflect our deepest longings, a role for which we have specific gifting, has only intensified my second-guessing. If I were really called to teach, would I still feel nervous stepping into the classroom? If I were called to teach, would I still be literally sweating my way through my professional writing class, dizzy with relief when each day is done because I've somehow made it to the end? If God wanted me to teach, wouldn't I be less fearful, less uncertain, less suspicious that, twenty-some years into my career, someone will unmask me as a fraud?

Because we often understand calling as an immutable decision we make in early adulthood, and because we understand calling as primarily vocational, we exert certain pressure not only on young adults, but also on ourselves. This is also true when our vocational choices have included parenthood. I've watched friends who made child-rearing their primary vocation struggle to define themselves when their nests become empty, the particular calling to meet the day-to-day needs of their children no longer pressing. One woman, whose kids are eighteen and twenty, realized that her answer to the question "What do you do?" was no longer apropos, since "stay at home" mom didn't really describe her role when her kids were no longer home. Like countless others, she was faced with the follow-up question: "Now that your kids are out of the house, what's next for you?"

Sound familiar?

Turns out, when young adults are trying to figure out what's next for their lives, we are too, many of us casting about again for what we are called to do. Worrying that our confusion and doubt and questions might mean we have not yet discovered the work to which God has called us. Praying that this pathway might be made clear, and then wondering what God's seeming silence really means.

If pressed, I imagine most of us might agree that the language of calling is too narrow. That Scripture itself urges us to understand calling beyond its vocational impulses. That different callings are not only announced in the Gospels, but emulated in the life and ministry of Jesus himself. Indeed, the Gospels talk very little about Jesus' vocational calling to be a carpenter, and instead narrate a far more expansive understanding of calling. Jesus says that we should love God, and love one another. Jesus calls us to mercy, to peacemaking, to kindness: for those who manifest these actions are considered blessed. He calls us to live simply, to reject wealth by selling our possessions and providing for the poor. In this, Jesus urges an entirely different understanding of calling than one that ensures financial security and prestige!

Emma gave language to this sense of calling, affirming that when we think about calling differently, "we get to see the creativity of the Spirit and our God-given uniqueness." We should endeavor, she said, to focus our attention on "the calls of Christ to love all and care for the marginalized, the call to share his hope with others, the call to live lives of holiness and sacrifice." I wonder how our relationships with young adults, and our ability to mentor them well, would shift if we were to embrace this spacious definition of calling, one rooted in Jesus' love for us and our love for each other. I wonder how *we* would be transformed by that same understanding. I wonder whether I would feel the same deep thrums of insecurity if I believed that God's call on my life was not to be a superstar professor, but rather someone who fervently seeks only to love God, and to love my neighbor as myself.

Helping young adults find their vocation is still important. But there are ways to do this mentoring well. The first step is to revise expectations for young adults, refusing to believe or affirm those cultural scripts that outline what a successful life will look like, for us and for the young people we cherish. We might need to decide that college—and especially college at eighteen—is not the first step every person must take to adulthood; or that those attending college should not immediately choose a major that promises a lucrative career, rather than pursuing a liberal arts education that has the potential to make them better thinkers, communicators, and world citizens. Encouraging young adults to seek opportunities and experiences that deepen their appreciation for human nature, whether through travel or service industry jobs or volunteering with national organizations, might help them taste the vast array of options available to them.

And letting them fail once in a while helps young adults see more clearly what they don't want to spend their lives doing. I'm grateful that my parents cheered my year in voluntary service after college, rather than forcing me to start a moneymaking career, because it showed me areas for which I have little aptitude; after that, staying in their basement and trying retail, without the pressure to establish a lifelong vocation, allowed me to eliminate an entire industry from my career aspirations. These failures were ultimately just as instructive as the roles in which I succeeded, a reminder to me that letting my kids try different pathways, and hit dead ends, can be useful.

Much more significantly, though, giving young adults freedom to explore may allow them to know the many ways to which we are called, beyond vocation alone. That might mean supporting them financially, if we're able; or encouraging them to work instead of taking out school loans; or helping them see calling as less about finding a profitable career and more about becoming the person God calls them to be, in all the ways God calls us.

In *Traveling Mercies*, Anne Lamott writes about her longing for assurance that the people she loves will continue to thrive, that they will not face illness or pain, that they will find their way forward into a settled life. She recognizes that God cannot provide us any such guarantees, and that all we really have is "the moment, and the imperfect love of people."[4] This might be at the heart of our work as parents and mentors, patiently accepting what each day will bring, holding our hands open to receive the imperfect love of the people we imperfectly love, without the expectation that they—or we—will have a clear sense of what happens next, save for God's tender mercy.

What will we do with the life we're given? Is it possible to acknowledge that we are called, all of us, to a beautiful life completely divorced from our vocations? How might our own lives model for young adults an openness to the moment, rather than angst about finding our next productive role? How can we embrace the simple rhythms of daily living, of accepting the gift of each day without deciding we need to know our calling beyond loving God and loving each other?

I'm not sure how to answer these questions. But I'm learning how to hold on to the unknowing of what each day might bring. I hope you'll live in that tension as well, alongside the young adults you love. And together, we will find our way forward, aware of God's perfect love for us and the understanding that God calls us to so much more than finding that one sweetly static spot where Buechner writes that "the world's deep hunger" and our own "deep gladness" will meet.

SHORT EXERCISES

1. Consider your own circuitous path to adulthood. What or who influenced your decisions as a young adult around vocation, schooling, your future? What advice would you have given your younger self?

2. Think about the advice you've offered the young adults in your life. Have you insisted that they settle on a vocational pathway? What drives that insistence?

3. How can you best support the young people in your life as they figure out who God has created them to be? What are specific, direct actions you can take to lend this support?

THREE

Through Lament

The **"cry and goodbye"** is a ritual every fall at my university, occurring during first-year orientation a few days before the semester starts. Families gather in our quad for one final meeting with the campus pastors, who provide last-minute counsel during a candle-lighting ceremony. Students then scatter across the green space to say farewell to their families.

Our quad is a tsunami of tears, moms and dads hugging their children, sobbing, trying to absorb the last few moments of child-rearing before a goodbye that signals the end of an era: eighteen or more years of meeting their kids' needs, knowing their (almost) every move, making decisions for their kids, sometimes for good, sometimes not. A colleague describes unwittingly walking into the quad during the cry and goodbye ceremony and feeling a wall of grief surround her. It was so palpable she turned back to her office rather than wade through the sorrow.

The pain of farewell is that heavy, and when I watched from the perch of my office building steps each year, I knew that pain was coming for me. One day I would be the parent, holding tightly to my kids, not wanting to let them go. In the last few years before my sons turned eighteen, I couldn't even watch anymore. It was too sad.

When Benjamin matriculated at George Fox in fall 2020, COVID altered first-year orientation, including this crucial, tearful event. Although there was no corporate worship service, campus pastors asked us to meet in the quad with our children, offering a handout with guided discussion questions to share with our kids about what we dreamed for their futures, as well as what we identified as the gifts they brought to campus.

My husband and Benjamin and I sat at a picnic table outside my office building, under the trees where the boys had once played, where they'd learned to ride their bikes, where they waited for me to finish office hours after their school days so we could drive home together. Both Ron and I tried completing the instructions we'd been given by our campus pastors, but I was crying too hard, unable to even speak. This felt like too much, a rending of my heart that rendered me speechless. We held hands, and prayed, and hugged Ben, and told him goodbye, then retreated to my office to cry some more while Ben walked back to his dorm to begin his journey alone. My tears contributed to the tsunami, and I felt a kinship with all the other parents, on our campus and elsewhere, releasing their children to a future we'd still be a part of, but in a different way entirely.

Later that evening, Ben called. He'd packed only one sock. Not one pair of socks, but a single, solitary sock. Could I please gather up some socks he'd left in his room at home? Or even better, could I buy him some new socks and deliver them to his dorm in the morning? I laughed at the absurdity of it all: that my kid would pack only one sock for college, his preparation so arbitrary and scattered because we lived ten minutes from the campus where Ron and I worked. It also felt like Ben was miles and miles away from home.

Ben's life had been so intricately tied to mine for eighteen years, and then it was not. How are we supposed to carry on after this uncoupling? Some days, I still don't know.

I'm grieving the passage of time: all those child-raising years behind us, as well as everything those years held. When our kids are young, most every parent hears some version of "Time goes so fast!" and "Enjoy them while they're little because before you know it, they'll be grown up." Some days, that sensibility seemed impossible, my patience worn thin by a tedious afternoon spent watching my boys climb around the playground, or freezing myself stiff at a kid-pitched base-ball game that went into extra innings. Those days dragged by in slow motion, and I couldn't wait until bedtime so I could have half an hour to watch television or read a book in peace.

For most parents, the years between when we meet our kids and when they launch into the world stretch long, until they don't, until we are watching them reach for their high school diploma and eye their exit into adulthood. We've all spent so much time meeting our children's every need, their lives the planets around which we orbit, making decisions based pri-marily if not solely on what will be best for them. Choices about work, about vacations, about how we spend our free time and our money are guided by the families we've created, and as a parent, it can seem like we spend several decades deflecting our own needs for the sake of our kids. My mom ate the burnt toast, the dregs in the soup pot, the last crusted sliver of cheese so my siblings and I could have the good stuff. Maybe she took the self-sacrifice of parenting too far, but she modeled for me a selflessness I knew I needed to assume in my own life, for my sons' first eighteen years at least.

Sure, the universe expands as young people become teenagers, as their attention turns from us to their friends and to their future. Kids can also be occasional monsters in the throes of adolescence, and we may pine for the days when they are finally out of the house for good, no longer causing chaos, no longer needing to face the embarrassment of their parents' simple existence. Even then, even in the slammed doors, the assurance that we are indeed ruining their lives by making them get jobs or come home at midnight or avoid toxic friendships: even then, many parents remain the grounding element, the home our kids can safely return to when they insist they'd rather be somewhere else entirely.

Now that my family is past all those years, I lament that those days are gone, that we won't even experience the volatility again, because that also means we won't enjoy all those other moments too. Driving home from soccer practice with the hard beats of Sam's music making the windows hum because he wanted to share a new song. Planning a trip to H-Mart and Powell's Books with Ben, what he once termed "love day," so that we could buy books and Vietnamese snacks. Taking a short road trip to see their nephews, and watching the little boys crawl all over my teen sons, Enzo and Mateo enthralled that their cool uncles would be staying the weekend.

I want to shake the younger me awake, tell her to pay attention, to lean deep into each moment with my sons. The silence in our home, our empty nest, calls into question the past twenty years. What was I doing with my time? Was I even there? I cry out for the time I lost, for the hours and days and years when I thought the future wouldn't come, that somehow my kids would be perpetually ten, scrawny and laughing and always moving and exhausting.

My tears are a collective grief shared by people through-out time, those saying goodbye in campus quads and in air-ports and on front lawns, watching their children drive off to a future that won't necessarily include them, or at least not in the same way. Standing in the quad, hugging my grown-older son, ties me to every other parent who has likewise stood in that space, relinquishing their children to the unknown—including my parents, who said farewell to me at the same campus thirty-some years earlier.

Grieving the end of an era seems entirely natural—neces-sary, even. Yet we are often embarrassed by our sadness. In the days after my sons left home the second time, one to enter the Navy and the other for a job in Colorado, I avoided talking about them with others, well aware that any conversations about Ben and Sam might devolve into tears. (That I used the word *devolve* in the previous sentence reflects my unease with emotional expression, with the grief I was feeling.)

Celebrating an empty nest seems impossible when your heart is breaking. Some might diagnose this heartbreak as unhealthy, as an unwillingness to let go. Even when life as we know it is over, when the people we love say goodbye to childhood, we often don't know what to do with our grief, nor how to explore the contours of our sadness. But what if we recognized lament as a response very much rooted in the deep love we have for young people in our lives? How might staying in that grief, rather than working so hard to "get over" our sadness, help us find our way forward with the young adults we love?

If we simply suggest that all is well when our kids leave home—that, in fact, we rejoice in their absence from our homes—we circumvent the opportunity to fully experience the love we have for them, as well as to know God's deep love for us reflected in our children. Lament provides us an honest reckoning with a shift in our lives, compelling us to realize we can't ever go back to the way things were. Rather than just moving straight to a new normal, we might do well to honor what causes us to mourn and create rituals which acknowledge that sadness itself is sacred.

One of many things my university's spiritual life office has gotten right is creating the cry-and-goodbye ceremony for parents and children, lending weight to the grief of separation by ritualizing it. Other kinds of goodbyes might also benefit from intentionality, like sharing a meal before departure, or praying together in a loved one's new apartment. Simply brushing tears aside and being unwilling to share our grief may only complicate it, rather than allowing us and the young adults we love the opportunity to explore its depths and be transformed. If grieving is one way to express love—our love for our children, and God's expansive love to us all—why would we want to suppress these tears?

Most eighteen-year-olds don't mourn quite as much. Oh, sure, at the cry-and-goodbye, some children weep into their parents' shoulders. I can still recall one young man, standing at the edge of campus with his father, sobbing while his father held him. They'd found a fairly secluded place to say their farewells, and the image of those two men there, alone with each other, has stayed with me so many years because of its poignancy. My own sons showed far fewer tears—none, actually—when we said our goodbyes. My youngest pulled back from a hug to ask me if I'd be okay, because I was so obviously distraught by his parting. I will be okay, I gulped. I doubt my reassurance was convincing.

But yes: for most young people, this separation from their parents is something they've anticipated for years, part of the normal stage of human development when they individuate, becoming their own people. They're ready for whatever happens next, and in this liminal space between being a child and being an adult, the world is opening up to them. Perhaps it's the precariousness of this space that seems so delightful for young people, yet so fraught to parents. They are neither child nor fully adult, oscillating and unmoored between two definitive life stages. Legally, by many definitions in the United States, they are now adults, and can make adult decisions about voting, marriage, independent living, and military enlistment. These milestones serve as significant markers, and most eighteen-year-olds consider themselves adults. After all, they've heard for years about this transitive moment when they magically enter adulthood, when life is immeasurably better and freer after their oppressive teenage years.

Becoming an adult doesn't happen in a flash, of course. Instead, our body and brain continue to transform after we turn eighteen, and our cultural markers of adulthood don't fully acknowledge this reality: that our brains, including the frontal lobe, the part of our brain used for decision-making, don't fully develop until we are twenty-five. According to Sandra Aamodt, author of *Welcome to Your Child's Brain*, young people continue experiencing brain development through their teens and early twenties, and when they are eighteen, their brains are about halfway to full maturity. The frontal lobe not only guides decisions, but also controls impulsiveness, and helps us organize our lives in such a way to meet goals. Aamodt suggests that the young adult years are more precarious than when people are teens because young adults are more willing to take impulsive risks and make impetuous choices just when we are releasing them to a world without the same guardrails, the same levels of adult supervision.[1]

The gutted feeling some of us experience when we say goodbye to young adults we love might reflect what we know viscerally: that we are releasing them into a world without the best tools for navigation, including a fully formed brain. The time until they have grown brains stretches longer, and we might be tempted to despair.

Author Christina Fox notes that Scripture consistently addresses the emotion of fear, perhaps no more so than in the Psalms, which can echo the singer's despair, animated by fear. The psalmist cries out to God, seeking deliverance from pain and from enemies who persecute the writer, and who have "brought him low" (see, for example, Psalm 142). But according to Fox, these psalms of lament reflect God's invitation to express our fears, opening our hearts and minds to remember God's faithfulness and to trust that God loves us, that God will ultimately deliver us from that which threatens us.[2] This does not mean we should turn from lament—that is not the case at all. Instead, allowing ourselves to lament our separation from our children, our fears for them, and the passing of a life we once had opens up space for us to see and know God better. In writing about the psalms of lament, theologian Howard Macy affirms that

> to learn from the psalmists' laments the ways of honesty, trust, and patience helps us when we are caught in despair. But even these, as useful as they are, supply neither easy formulae nor instant cures. There are none. Struggles will come. We'll be tempted to choose pious sham over truth. We may stammer our confessions of trust. Our cries for help may sound more pushy than patient. Yet for those that know God, that is not the whole story. The pulse of the Creator's heart resonates in the secret chambers of our own, so that we know somehow, deeply, that despair is not the last word.[3]

When we feel ashamed of our sadness, hiding in platitudes about the empty nest or asserting a joy in freedom we don't really cherish, because "the joy of the Lord is our strength" and "I have complete trust in God's will for my kids," we are choosing the pious sham about which Macy writes. The truth might be far more complicated, because we are all complicated people. Expressing our grief—that we miss our children, that we fear for their future, and for ours—might allow us an honest reckoning with what we've lost, with the years now behind us. And in our lament, we open ourselves up to connect with others: with those who are likewise grieving, for sure; but also with those for whom we're grieving, and who might one day interpret in our tears the deep love we have for them, a love so expansive it brings us to our knees, literally and figuratively.

I hope my lament also reflects my willingness to fully release my kids into the world, to be loved and cherished by others too.

But this world right now? This world seems like a mess.

I mean this in an existential sense, but also literally: the earth itself seems in shambles, the accumulating impact of climate change causing outsize natural disasters that threaten every region of the globe. No place feels entirely safe, and even here in Oregon's notoriously moderate climate, our summers are hotter, with drought plaguing parts of a state and yearly forest fires encroaching even closer to heavily populated areas. While politicians dither about what should be done, while scientists sound warnings, the world burns, and some young people must wonder whether there will be a habitable planet left for them when they reach full adulthood. We are called to mourn this unhealthy earth, as well as the unwillingness of so many to chart a different path away from climate crises.

A once-in-a-century global pandemic has also upended everything, compelling us to make risk calculations about even the simplest acts like sitting in a coffee shop or attending church. COVID-19 has complicated young adults' lives immeasurably, robbing them of some important, long-anticipated milestones. My sons' loss of a traditional high school graduation seemed a loss worth grieving, until we recognized that the pandemic had robbed other young people of family members who caught the virus and died; or economic security, since neither they nor their parents could work; or

even—for those young people who now have long COVID—
the loss of a healthy future. Given these challenges, receiving
a high school diploma from the front seat of our Mazda was a
minor inconvenience, but still worth mourning. Like others,
we missed so many of life's rituals—proms, graduations, weddings, birthday parties. We are called to mourn the loss of so
much, including time celebrating together with loved ones.

Deepening ideological divisions not only in the United
States, but also worldwide, are also worth mourning, as ever
more extremist political positions seem increasingly main-
stream. The summer of protests that followed George Floyd's
murder in May 2020 amplified the need for racial reckoning in the United States, revealing the unwillingness of some
to accept the ways that systemic racism is woven into the
very fabric of our country and its beginnings. Some govern-
ment leaders are unwilling to condemn the inflamed rhetoric of white nationalist groups—and indeed, these leaders
are sometimes voicing similar nativist language that further
imperils the lives and livelihood of Black, brown, Indigenous,
and LGBTQIA individuals and communities. Media compa-
nies are complicit in fueling these divisions, allowing disinformation to metastasize, destroying families and friendships,
because we cannot agree on the nature of truth, or the difference between fact and opinion. Young people today are being
launched into a world that feels angrier, more chaotic, and
more unsafe than at any point in living memory. Through all
of this, we are called to mourn the absence of peace in our
communities.

Trying to launch into independence is also more complicated than ever, thanks to the dearth of affordable housing in
most US communities as well as inflation and a gig economy

that makes most entry-level jobs precarious, most entry-level employees expendable. A shortage of apartments and rental homes means young adults have to make difficult choices between the high cost of independence and moving back home to save on rent; in late 2021, almost half of all eighteen- to thirty-four-year-olds were living with at least one parent.[4] Many who attended college have the additional burden of paying back costly student loans, another stressor affecting countless young adults who may feel that their financial future is bleak, the American dream they are still told to seek forever out of reach. Those who decide to enter the workforce at eighteen also face challenges, the jobs available to them rarely paying enough to allow for complete independence from their parents.

The young people I've talked to acknowledge the many stressors they face now as they enter adulthood, even as expectations about what it means to be successful persist. Many of those raised in Christian homes have the added cultural messages about marriage and family and what it means to be blessed by God. Some Christians also encounter the corrosive effects of the prosperity gospel in their churches and homes, and they struggle to deem their young adulthood a success because they don't have presumed markers of God's providence in their lives: a partner, a lucrative job, and a mortgage (or at least their own apartment).

We are called to mourn all these stressors and more—and to allow the young adults we love this mourning too.

I know too well what it means to shut down my sons' sadness. When their high school closed two months before graduation, I remained upbeat, reminding them of all they wouldn't have to navigate at the school year's end, the banquets and parties and silly rituals like prom they could avoid. We celebrated together that they would graduate with their class, the pandemic canceling the final exams they would have needed to pass to be eligible for graduation. Heck, I even wrote a cheery article about their drive-through graduation for a national publication, happy that I didn't have to shiver through long valedictory speeches on a late-spring Oregon evening, when it can be damp and cold even in June.[5]

We might be tempted to tell young adults to wait: that the world will find a new normal in which they can thrive. This sentiment offers little comfort when the here and now feels so fraught, when they might all be questioning whether there will be a world waiting for them once their brains have fully developed. Insisting they wait for a new normal is one more way we try to circumvent lament, papering over the pain and trauma of the past few years in an effort to make everything seem right with the world.

Because let's face it. We who are to serve as mentors and guides to young adults are also surviving in unprecedented times, staring into the unknown without much assurance that we're doing right by the young people in our lives. Many of the usual navigational tools we used throughout our kids' lives have disappeared, replaced by social isolation and the general sense of upheaval caused by the past few years. Even when I was shivering on the sidelines of my kids' baseball games, I was processing parenthood with other moms in the stands, and this community carried me through middle and high school: the sport may have changed, but I still found like-minded people on the sidelines eager to share their stories and help me understand my sons. That sideline companionship mostly disappears when our kids graduate and scatter, and the pandemic exacerbated the already diminished encounters with people we might have seen on the regular for a decade or more.

Many of us are also facing multiple losses while existing in a world we might not wholly recognize, a world far different from the one we walked through as young adults. My husband lost his teaching job mere weeks after my sons graduated high school, and we were suddenly faced with a lost income plus the loss of a vocation my husband had pursued and loved deeply for nearly thirty-five years. Trying to launch our sons into adulthood while also grieving this loss proved exceedingly difficult, and yet we were not alone. Some people are grieving the loss of the people they loved. Some are grieved because of increased threats of racial violence in their communities. And some are mourning the loss of children to that violence.

When we are hurting and feeling the lack of the support structures we've relied on, figuring out how to successfully launch kids into adulthood seems even more difficult. At one time, I might have turned to the legion of books about parenthood as a guide, or to the cascade of mommy blogs that provided a kind of lodestar through my kids' early years. Even those resources tend to diminish as our kids grow older and mom bloggers realize their teens would rather not have their most embarrassing moments broadcast to middle-aged readers looking for comic relief. Most days, it can feel like we are white-knuckling this parenting stage without any kind of guardrails, and without the presence of traveling companions cheering us on, reminding us that our complex emotions are normal—especially in unprecedented times.

I want so badly for my sons to be settled right now, to have clear insight into who they will become and how they will handle the impetuous world they will face. Much as I want this assurance, I've tried to step into the mystery of tomorrow, asking God to help me rejoice in the unknown of my sons'— and my own—futures, as well as the known of their pasts. I've even taken to praying at times with my palms open, hoping to receive wisdom about how I can best mentor my sons and my students when I believe myself lost. But still. Some days, I want to be told exactly what my next step should be: How to teach a face-to-face class on writing in the middle of a pandemic. How to reach students struggling with mental health challenges that keep them pinned to their beds with anxiety, unable to attend class. How to address the pernicious nature of social media. How to talk about racism and misogyny in settings fraught with fears about recrimination. Heck, I want someone to tell me how often it's okay to call my sons, now living in other states, and whether I should panic when they go a week without texting me a funny meme.

How to guide others into the future seems impossible when we ourselves feel lost. Still, perhaps we should start by lamenting all that we've lost. All that others have lost. All that can be lost if we don't do the work needed to create a more just and equitable world for future generations.

There are plenty of reasons to lament, not least of which is our young people growing up, leaving home, our lives passing too quickly, our obsolescence coming too soon. To be sure, our lament is embedded with privilege and with historical shortsightedness. There have been other pandemics (the Black Plague wiped out almost half of Europe's population, and only a century ago, the Great Influenza killed, by some estimates, one hundred million people). Every historical epoch has had its share of human suffering. Even now, image bearers of our Creator are dying in genocides and starving because of drought and facing the constant threat of bombs being dropped onto their children's schoolyards.

Still, this has been a stretch of years when every day brings more bad news. Sometimes, I try hard to ignore social media because I know that Twitter will bring me news of one more tragedy, one more new way that humans have been inhumane, one more example of when power has corrupted God's people. It seems like the world is spinning into chaos, and we might be inclined to echo the psalmist: "My God, my God, why have you forsaken me? Why are you so far from helping me, from the words of my groaning? O my God, I cry by day, but you do not answer; and by night but find no rest" (Psalm 22:1–2 NRSVue). At times, it seems like we are running headlong into the world's ending, or toward the end of civil society, or here in the United States, into the end of our democracy.

The Bible's narrative arc reminds us that lament gives way to hope, that mourning will be replaced by joy. In Psalm 22, the poet's grief yields to rejoicing in the recognition that God has not forsaken him, that God's providence reigns, that the poor will not be hungry forever and the downtrodden will find God's favor. The resurrection story itself announces that the lament on Good Friday prepares us for the joy of Jesus' return, of life conquering death. Without the bitter agony of the crucifixion, we would not have the luminous good news of Easter Sunday.

Lament isn't the end of our story.

Since time's beginning, young people have left their families behind, doing the developmentally normal act of individuating and finding independence. When I've felt especially sad about the geographical distance separating me from my children, I'm inclined to castigate myself: *You think you have it bad?* my unkind self says. *Previous generations didn't have FaceTime or text. They sent their kids away across oceans and prairies and never saw them again. Suck it up, buttercup.* Instead of hiding my tears and insisting I be okay with this dramatic transition in my life, though, I wonder how much better it would be to linger in lament, expressing my deep sadness for what has been and what will be, as well as accepting my despair for the many horrors that continue in the here and now.

Theologian Eugene Peterson writes that "a failure to lament is a failure to connect," arguing that in attempting to avoid sadness, we "choose to distance ourselves from our experience, and compromise our intimacy with God."[6] Pastor and professor Soong-Chan Rah observes, "Lament will not allow us to revert to easy answers. There is no triumphalistic and exceptionalistic narrative that can cover up justice. There are no easy answers to unabated suffering. Lament continues."[7] These two notions should inform the heart of our lives with young people. Expressing deep sadness about their absence reflects the profound love we have for them and the longing for their presence in our lives. Acknowledging the challenges we are all facing means an honest reckoning with the many unjust forces that have caused today's horrors, rather than using triumphalist cant about God's will and God's control to cover our sorrow. In other words, we need to sit in our sadness and lament, and then go about the work of justice, assuring the world will be a better place for our children, for *all* children.

This life offers no guarantees. Perhaps this is what's so unsettling: our young people have agency to make of their lives what they want—and sometimes, a once-in-a-century pandemic, or a housing crisis, or a country's racial violence can send someone spinning off course, no matter what we do. We want so badly to know the future, to control the outcome of our decades-long commitment to help our children reach adulthood and our efforts to make a more just world. Instead, what we get is uncertainty, and maybe—if we're lucky—a phone call now and then letting us know they're currently doing well, or that they need more socks. Nevertheless, we should lament. And then, from the anguish of our souls, persist in making a better tomorrow, where God is sovereign.

SHORT EXERCISES

1. Reflect on a time when you had to say goodbye to a young adult you love. Describe the thoughts and feelings you had then. Did you give yourself time to lament the ending of this period in your life? How could you make space for mourning now?

2. Consider writing a psalm of lament. If you need models to emulate, here are a few you can read: Psalms 6, 22, 38, 130.

3. How can you transform your mourning about the world right now? Try to come up with three action steps you might take to change your mourning to activism, creating a more just and equitable world for all young adults.

FOUR

Alone and Together

As a new college graduate, I often purchased a day-long ticket for Seattle transit. Bus tickets were inexpensive, and I was friendless in Seattle and craving human contact. It didn't matter where I went, and sometimes I jumped on a bus without consulting a schedule, just to see where it might take me: through the university district, along the Puget Sound, into downtown. The destination wasn't the point. I just needed to be near people because I was stuck in a job and in a house that left me alone most of the time. Faithfully an introvert, I rarely talked to anyone on the bus. Being near others, though; and watching them interact; and looking at sky-high apartment blocks, imagining the rich lives of those inhabited there: that I could buy with just a few bucks. A Saturday spent riding a bus around Seattle meant one more weekend when I wasn't wholly alone, even though I wasn't really with anyone either.

I ached with loneliness.

Several months later, I moved to Pittsburgh, lured away from Seattle by the promise of community, friendship, maybe even a romantic relationship with someone who wrote me plaintive letters, which I unfolded and read over and over again in my Seattle basement, the only lifeline I felt then to a living, breathing human. Days into my thousands-mile move to Pittsburgh, though, I discovered that long-distance letters can construct a mirage of a person who is different in real life. Heck, *minutes* into my move, I realized that letters cannot always help you know someone, and that it's possible to build a persona through writing that is vastly different from the honest-to-God man standing in front of you. He was someone I knew, kind of, and not some stranger on the bus. This initially seemed like an improvement, an upgrade where human relationships were concerned.

My aching loneliness was temporarily blunted by his presence, though as the year progressed, I realized that post-college, finding real friendships was hard. Up until that point in my life, developing friendships had been second nature, thanks to school, sports teams, and all those ready-made structures that put into my orbit same-aged peers who at least shared some interests. Now, out in the world, finding people my age, let alone ones whom I liked, was exceedingly more difficult.

No one had prepared me for the loneliness of adulthood: not back then, when graduation scattered my social groups; not now, when my kids' graduation from high school also reordered my life, making it less likely for me to connect with other parents, my primary friend circle for the past twelve years. While I'm not riding buses anymore to slake my loneliness, I am well aware that isolation is a common thread tying our young people to each other, and to the adults in their lives, as we all experience similar pangs of loneliness.

We are together in spirit, but also so alone.

Young people have spent most of their lives surrounded by same-aged peers, and while friendships during school aren't always uncomplicated, most of us find at least some connection in our K–12 classrooms, in after-school activities, in sports teams and theater departments and music programs. For some, the transition from a rich social life to loneliness happens after high school, when they enter the workforce and find the pattern of day-to-day interaction with other young people diminished. For some, the transition happens after college, when four years of communal dining and dorm life give way to eating alone and sleeping in a solitary bedroom, sometimes in an apartment, sometimes back in the family home.

This stage of human development also complicates young adults' deep connection with others. During their late teens and early twenties, people are trying to figure out their identity: a sense of who they are and where they belong in their world. Old alliances with childhood friends might dissipate as identities shift, causing inner turmoil. People may wonder why the companions with whom they shared every part of life no longer bear any resemblance to the friends they once were. I watched this shift in my younger son, and it was heartbreaking to witness—his best friend for a decade stopped coming to our house as their interests and friend groups diverged. Heartbreaking for me, I should say, but less so for my child, for whom this shift was a natural developmental phase.

Young adults consistently hear that they are in the "best time of their lives," and that they should make the most of their youth. Persistent messaging in the media only exacerbates the sense that young adults are well connected, with ample friend groups around for weekend parties, trips to the beach, late-night hangouts in upscale bars. The television show *Friends* did for my generation what other shows, like *New Girl*, have done for younger generations, defining expectations for what it means to be young and independent and living in edgy apartments, surrounded by like-minded peers who enjoy hanging out together each evening after working satisfying daytime jobs. Few shows convey the reality of being a young adult, when a less than ideal daytime job causes ennui that makes it impossible to get off the couch in a cramped studio apartment, let alone hang with friends who have scattered.

Social media has intensified these expectations of a richly connected life. By now, most of us are savvy navigators of social platforms, and Gen Z people are the savviest of all. They've had smartphones for much of their upbringing, joining social media platforms the moment they turned thirteen, if not earlier. Most also recognize that social media offers curated images and does not accurately reflect real life, and that their peers make intentional choices about the public personas they cultivate for their followers. Startling reports about the dangers of social media haven't really curtailed use, and some studies show that people rely heavily on apps like Instagram even when they are aware of the apps' corrosive impact on their mental health.

And so, even though young people know that social media posts are often just a mirage, seeing one's like-aged peers out having fun with large groups of friends can't help but intensify a sense of isolation. When social media posts make it seem like everyone else is leading a rich, fulfilling life with workmates, fantastic parties, and perhaps a significant other, those who feel lonely might decide to isolate even more, ashamed that their own complicated existence doesn't measure up. This can create a cycle of shame and isolation from which it is difficult to extract oneself. Carla Manly, a psychologist and the author of *Joy from Fear*, says that those who are lonely struggle to admit as much to others, choosing isolation because they fear the stigma of loneliness; in turn, this makes them lonelier. Social apps like Tinder feed this cycle by conditioning young people to see relationships as something established instantaneously, a quick right or left swipe deciding whether someone is worth getting to know.[1] Faced with the complicated dance that can characterize the beginnings of some friendships, the slow pace at which we learn to know others, isolation sometimes seems less onerous.

Back when I was a recent graduate, sitting alone in my basement apartment and acutely missing my college friends, the US post and costly long-distance phone calls provided a tenuous connection to my past and to the people who mattered most in my life. I wanted so much more, but in a time before smartphones, I could only imagine all the other young people having a vibrant social life, so unlike the isolation I was experiencing. I thought about my friends still in college, enjoying campus without me; I envied those engaged or married or who otherwise had live-in companionship to keep them company. Now, I wonder how the internet and social media might have complicated my loneliness, making me feel even worse—how filtered photos of beautiful friends out together, or gazing lovingly at their partners, might have made my life seem significantly bleaker than it actually was. At the time, I couldn't have fathomed tools that put me immediately in touch with others, inexpensively, through a digital screen. But I also wouldn't have dreamed about all the ways that smartphones, apps, and other such technology exacerbate loneliness, making people feel even more isolated.

Instead of seeing social media as a positive connector that draws people together across time, we should acknowledge that the internet has dramatically influenced our sense of connection, and of isolation. I also wonder how we can help young people see that the time after high school, or after college, carries with it an unforeseen complication, given the lack of structures to put them in immediate proximity to likeminded, same-aged peers. Conveying that your twenties are always a rip-roaring good time, populated with tight friendships and ample connection, doesn't prepare young people for a reality that can leave them isolated and ashamed. Sure, graduation from high school or college might seem like a gateway to a much richer life, and I note in my students an eagerness to leave the small confines of Newberg, Oregon, for the abundance they imagine waiting out there. But I wonder whether they should also be prepared for an unfortunate reality. Sometimes, finishing school looks like riding a transit bus alone or working solo in a studio apartment while desperate for human interaction, which is where my nephew found himself after graduation, working remotely and keenly missing the rich social life that had carried him through college.

My own social life hadn't been quite as rich during college, but I somehow knew that the relationships I'd fostered in four years of school would be hard to replicate in the world outside of college, especially as people around me started to put down roots, marrying and starting families, shifting their priorities. For many, this natural progression toward a settled life means that by their late twenties, people report feeling less alone, having nurtured communities or found partners who provide them with human connection. Still, surveys completed in the United States and in Britain suggest that those in their twenties experience loneliness far more acutely than those in any other life stage, save for the most elderly among us.[2] I imagine this information can be cold comfort for those just now embarking on adulthood, to know that for the next decade at least, the sadness of being alone might linger. Nor do these studies account much for those who remain unpartnered, by choice or circumstance, and whose isolation might well continue as those around them find companionship in a romantic relationship, and beyond that, possibly in raising children.

Literature about the nature of friendship and of family often galls me because of this simple oversight: not everyone finds lovely people with whom to share community. It's presumptuous to assume that young adults will find a suitable partner, that they will raise children, even that they will forge close friendships. Embedded in that presumption is the message that those who continue to feel isolated are at fault for their isolation, and if they would just *do something*—join a dating app, go to church, host a book group—their loneliness would end. I've read paeans to friendship with gritted teeth, angry at the lack of empathy for those who don't have close friends or a romantic partner, angry at the insinuation that every lonely person is making an intentional choice to remain alone.

Yet here's the truth: having a spouse and children did diminish the loneliness I felt. Not only because I had a ready-made cadre of people with whom I could interact, though that was important. Even on days when it was just me and infant Ben, I was far less isolated than when it was me alone. But having children naturally puts you into contact with other families, and as your kids grow, those other families can become community, if only because of proximity. Some of my closest friendships developed on the sidelines to my kids' activities, when we were all held captive by the necessity of presence. Needing to be somewhere, supervising our children, provided ample time to talk to other parents. Watching baseball, for example, pinned me to a lawn chair behind the dugout, fingers frozen in the Oregon spring, but with several hours to spare, I became friends with other mothers shivering beside me, and I looked forward to those games for the community it gave me.

There's unequal abundance in that too, of course, and I know not all parents experience such camaraderie, either because their children don't do extracurricular activities or because circumstances—like a sixty-hour work week or having children with disabilities that complicate socializing—make it difficult to attend kids' activities. But for many parents, those kinds of close friendships, focused on their children, continue and intensify through their child's middle and high school years until graduation, when consistent encounters with other parents can come to a grinding halt. I experienced this acutely because both my sons graduated, and then left home, at the same time. In their senior year, sensing the end was near, I signed up to volunteer for school activities, including planning a graduation party that never happened because of the pandemic. One moment I was strategizing with other parents to create a fabulous celebration for our kids, and then, in the months after their drive-through graduation, my connection began to wane, until I no longer saw my parent friends at all, unless I made intentional efforts to meet.

For parents whose calling has been stay-at-home care, the emptying of the nest can compound this sense of isolation. Without outside jobs that can provide connections with others, stay-at-home parents may find few opportunities to socialize while their primary identity simultaneously comes to an end. In one way, at least, parents everywhere can share this universal experience: when the nest empties, our homes can seem cavernous, lacking the energy and presence of children. That emptiness can extend beyond the nest too. The structures that put my kids in proximity to like-minded and like-aged peers paralleled the structures that allowed me to create and sustain friendships. Now that my sons are no longer living at home, I have far more time to meet others for lunch or a movie, but this requires planning and intention. There are fewer opportunities for casual conversation at the playground or a leisurely afternoon spent at a soccer game sideline, activities that required little planning but offered rich reward. Like the recent graduate who realizes that sustaining adult friendships takes effort, I've discovered that I also have to work to stay connected, and that sometimes it's far easier to watch Netflix alone in sweats than call up a friend and meet somewhere for dinner.

The coronavirus pandemic exacerbated this inertia for many of us, and so too the loneliness. Young adults especially felt the effects of social isolation, and numerous studies are just now emerging about how COVID has been most detrimental for those young adults. While those with immediate families could often hunker down with others in their households, some young adults lived alone or at a distance from their parents and siblings, compounding their loneliness. Others were just gaining traction in new communities when the pandemic hit, and lacked the social structures needed to create pods with other like-minded peers that might help alleviate isolation. And all the places that young people might congregate were also closed. Without bars, churches, social clubs, and gyms, it was far more difficult to meet and make friends, let alone sustain already established relationships.

The media's persistent willingness to blame young people for the spread of COVID contributed to the isolation that many young adults have experienced. After the first round of COVID-related shutdowns in 2020, media outlets started reporting on the indifference that young people were presumably exhibiting toward the illness, and toward the vulnerable who needed particular protection from disease. Headlines about young adults crowding into bars and "driving up coronavirus cases" implied that young people alone were to blame for the persistence of COVID contagion, their seeming across-the-board disregard for public health measures a reason to conclude that young adults were immoral and reckless. Instead of reckoning with the many losses they experienced at a time when they were seeking independence, including lost employment and canceled milestone moments and isolation, young adults had to contend with added scrutiny of their behavior. Judged as selfish and uncaring, willing to kill Grandma for a night out at a crowded bar, young adults faced an untenable choice: experience more isolation that could lead to considerable mental health challenges or risk the judgment of others who deemed them self-focused and immature. Faced with these options, it's no wonder that COVID made an already lonely time in the lives of young people even worse.

We are called to be a people of hope.

In Christian communities, the concept of hope is often applied to the idea of expectation: of waiting for a future that will somehow be better than the here and now. During Advent, we wait with hope through the darkest days of winter, anticipating the birth of Emmanuel, of God with us. At Easter, we talk about hope in the resurrection, symbolic in its triumph of life over death, good over evil. When we face challenges that push us to our knees by their force, we might express hope that someday, by the grace of God, our circumstances will be different.

To suggest that the lonely should live in hope seems almost facile, a too-easy prescription that does not account for the complexity of people's isolation and the difficulty of finding connection, given the contemporary barriers we face. At the same time, being called as a people to hope means acknowledging our isolation and being activated to seek out a different life for ourselves, one that includes the company of others.

And still, cliches abound. A student, writing about her own isolation, says she realized she's never really alone when she has her friend Jesus in her heart. Another mentions being so lonely at college that she wonders whether her experience will ever get better—*It must*, she acknowledges, *because this is the best time of my life.* Trying to convince herself, she is afraid that what she's feeling makes her an anomaly from her peers, who seem to have plenty of friends to sit with in the dining hall. A recent graduate tells me there's a lot to love about her apartment, and lacking a roommate doesn't much matter anyway, because introverts don't really need close friends, do they?

I don't know what to say, what antidote I can offer to their isolation, because I have ached with loneliness too. I still ache sometimes, when the house is empty and I'm staring down a weekend of Netflix and knitting and quiet dinners at the kitchen table, talking with my husband about our kids. *This is the time of your life*, the magazines tell me. *Rekindle your relationship with your spouse. Or with yourself.* Even these cliches don't remedy the yawning void in our lives now, with the kids away and the activities that once filled our weekends behind us. Because my stepdaughter has children, we are lucky—grandkids can partially fill that void, but that is not a panacea for everyone, nor even us. Our stepdaughter and her family live four hours away, and they have their own life. Like children, grandchildren grow up and cannot fulfill our every social need.

Prescriptions also don't help, not really. Do we really need more tightly packaged advice about how to make friends? Or the ten things every person should do to fight loneliness? While riding buses in Seattle, I knew what needed to happen: I needed to join clubs, find new activities, pursue a different hobby. I played in a volleyball league, and that helped, for a while. But like some medical prescriptions, this kind of advice only masks the problem that most of us experience. Whether you're a young adult or care about one, being lonely can come with the territory, especially because so many of us think we are alone in our loneliness.

This knowledge of our shared experience won't do much to cure the loneliness so many people encounter, but knowing that others are fighting similar isolation might make some of us feel a little less alone. There can be comfort and even connection in recognizing that others are on journeys parallel to our own. Being willing to tell others about the loneliness I've felt as an empty nester has not only been cathartic, but also helped me be more intentional about making connections with others. Even engaging with social media groups has helped—groups like Midlife Moms and Empty Nest, Full Life, moderated by Brenda Yoder and Jill Savage, respectively, connected me with others who dedicated the past few decades to raising children and who now find themselves in suddenly cavernous homes and wondering how to thrive alone or with their partners.

Acting with hope might mean destigmatizing loneliness. Because loneliness is stigmatized, and because it's often thought that the isolated have themselves to blame, few people want to admit that they are lonely. Cultural messaging reinforces shame around loneliness, not only with television shows portraying young adults having rich social lives, but also with predominantly negative representations of lonely people: as losers who cannot make friends, isolated by their incompetence and inability to relate to others. Despite statistics showing that loneliness is acute for young adults and for empty nesters, many keep their isolation hidden because of shame and the sense that something is fundamentally wrong with their personhood, making them unworthy of friendship and connection. That shame can create a cyclical pattern: fear of being deficient makes someone more lonely and thus more ashamed, which reinforces the sense of deficiency, as well as the incapacity to reach out and make connections with other people, thereby reinforcing loneliness.

Finding our way forward with young adults might mean being honest about times we've experienced loneliness, either when we were also young or now, when the life we've built around children no longer exists in the same way. Assuring others and ourselves that isolation is not something about which we should feel shame is significant, as is recognizing that no matter who we are or what we do, we are all inherently worthy of friendship and community. Being people of radical hope might mean believing that community and connection are available to us all, and that someday, our loneliness might be alleviated. It might also mean praying that such a day might come soon: for the young people we love, trying to find relationships in a sometimes unforgiving adult world; and for those of us seeking fellow travelers in the next part of our life journeys.

You probably heard the language of individuation countless times before your kids reached young adulthood. Back when they were in the toddler stage wanting to do everything for themselves—and, let's be honest, making any easy task take a hundred times longer—we were reassured that this independence was good, that our children were trying to individuate from us. As teenagers staking out agency and freedom from oppressive parenting, children are also individuating, pulling away from adults and all their awkward behaviors, like wearing the wrong clothes or breathing too heavily. In therapy sessions, when I expressed sadness about my teen sons' distance, their consistent preference for time with friends rather than family, I was reminded that this separation was developmentally appropriate, that I should rejoice in how *normal* my teen sons were.

"I know, I know," I wanted to say. "They're individuating. But do they have to be so obvious about it?" Since I try to be a nice person, I kept my irritated thoughts and deep eye rolls entirely interior, even if my therapist annoyed me with consistent reassurances about my kids' normality.

To some degree, individuation and loneliness are intertwined. Psychology tells us that solitude might even be crucial to individuation, and that only in our aloneness can we truly understand who we are and who we hope to be. Psychologist Carl Jung especially prized solitude as a significant way we get in touch with our truest selves. In adolescence, our kids' decisions to burrow into their bedrooms is, to some degree, developmentally normal as they figure out who they are apart from us. Although we're aware that's what they're doing, individuating can be painful for us, the parents, as the luxury of connection we enjoyed wanes and leaves us feeling even more isolated and alone. That continued individuation into young adulthood can be downright excruciating for parents; a longing for closeness with our children creates a visceral ache so intense we might delight in the crumbs of connection our kids give us: a one-word answer to texts, a TikTok video sent late at night.

In the year after my kids left home, I often wondered how much I should expect to hear from them. Moving from Newberg was invaluable for their individuation and maturity, and I rejoiced in their growth, all the while wishing my home didn't feel so quiet. Because I wanted them to have agency and independence, I vowed to let them make the first entries into communication, responding warmly when they wrote or called, but avoiding any persistent badgering via text or phone. That approach has worked, and I hear from both boys at least several times a week via text, with FaceTime every week or two, all initiated by them. But I wonder whether this contact is enough, and I can be envious of fellow moms who receive several messages each day from their young adults, or who proclaim their children their "best friends" with whom they spent significant time each week because they live close by or because they make efforts to visit.

Envy is the thief of joy, I know, and other parents have decidedly less contact with their kids than I do with mine and may mourn because their children are estranged or distant. Young people keep in touch with the adults in their lives with a varying range of frequencies, and it's easy to long for more, to believe that any connection is not nearly enough. In these moments—and I have them too, in spades—I try to assure myself that my children are individuating, an important development stage.

It also might be time for us to start becoming individuals apart from the young adults in our lives. Of course, I'm still Ben and Sam's mom, and always will be. But this transitory life stage should also offer new opportunity to become people apart from parenting roles, and to develop into who God has called us to be today. Without a doubt, this is incredibly hard work, and it starts with a premise similar to what we might tell our individuating and lonely children: we are all inherently worthy of connection and community, just as we are. After a lifetime of shame and stigma about loneliness, having that message break through might seem nearly impossible, despite the assurances from Scripture itself that as image bearers of our Creator, we are meant to be in community.

We might also need to reflect on some of that well-meaning advice, about how to make friends, how to stave off loneliness, even when that advice might seem daunting and a little too cloying. After my boys left home, I decided to try one small change in my behavior to assuage my isolation: I challenged myself to say yes to opportunities that, in years past, had been a definite no for me. This has meant stepping far outside my comfort zone: Going to a dance party, called Lady Sweat, with my stepdaughter. Agreeing to take students overseas for a three-week trip. Doing yoga on a stand-up paddleboard. Attending a late-night bluegrass concert in Portland when the show started long after bedtime. Playing pickleball. Joining a weird armada of kayaks and paddleboards on Halloween, traversing the Willamette River in witch costumes, a fundraiser for those experiencing houselessness in Portland. That adventure didn't make me any new besties (it was, in fact, rather miserable, paddling in late October!), but it was a different way to live life—and live it abundantly. And it definitely beat the alternative of staying in for another Saturday and streaming Netflix. Not that there's anything wrong with that either.

We are called to hope. To hope that tomorrow might be better than today, and that our current loneliness might be alleviated by authentic connection. Embracing hope might also mean persistently seeking community with others, even when our inclination is to isolate. Far more importantly, in my mind: for those who are not lonely, embracing hope might mean reaching out to others, using the privilege afforded by an already established community to pull someone else into your orbit, with the hope of expanding friendship beyond what is comfortable and secure.

Being called to hope might mean acknowledging our isolation and then, if we're able, saying yes to an opportunity we'd rather not take, awakened to the possibility of new friendship because all the old structures we've relied on no longer exist. Joining a community paddle event on Halloween might not yield new friendships, after all, but the experience can become an interesting story, one you can tell again and again until someone else thinks it might be a fun event to try with you next year. That right there is an example of the absurd hope to which we are sometimes called.

SHORT EXERCISES

1. Where and when have you felt a deep ache of loneliness? How can you use your experience with loneliness to connect with the young adults you love? After you reflect on the seasons of loneliness you've experienced, think about how you might start a conversation with a young adult about the nature of loneliness and its unfortunate connection to shame.

2. What are some activities you've said no to in the past, and why have you refrained from joining? Make a list of those activities and the reasons you said no, then pick one that might introduce you to new people. Promise to say yes to this activity and see what new perspectives—and maybe new friendships—this activity might yield.

3. What do you hope for your future, apart from the young adults in your life? Meditate on what your future might look like, and especially on what might bring you the most joy, apart from your already familiar relationships. What's keeping you from that future?

FIVE

By Walking Humbly

n April 2021, his college girlfriend sitting beside him and holding his hand, Benjamin told us he planned to enlist. He knew this conversation would be difficult for us, and needed her support, a young woman whose family had an entirely different appreciation for the military than his own.

He looked at me, sitting on the couch across the room, took a deep breath, and said it: "I've decided to leave George Fox." And then, "I'm enlisting in the Army."

My heart broke. My husband's heart broke. We spent several hours talking, crying, pleading for him to reconsider. And then the next few weeks. Talking. Crying. Pleading. Hoping he might make a different choice, return to college, forget about enlistment and what he saw as God's calling in his life.

His decision shocked me, though it wasn't really a surprise for me or Ron. This child of ours had dreamed about joining the military for years. At his adoption when Benjamin was seven months old, we learned that his caregivers had named him Do Minh Quan, which they told us meant soldier or warrior in Vietnamese. We retained Quan as his middle name, adding Benjamin to echo the Minh in his surname.[1] When he was old enough, he and I talked about why his caregivers might have called him Quan. In my imagination, he received the name because he was a fighter, his will to live overcoming a rough beginning as a preemie, including a three-month hospital stay and several blood transfusions. But Benjamin Quan believed his destiny as a soldier had been written at birth, manifest right there, in his name.

On a family trip to Pennsylvania, Ben, then six, wanted to spend time at Civil War memorials, studying the archaic weaponry encased by glass museum displays, undaunted by rows of gravestones at Gettysburg and Antietam. Several years later, and without prompting, he drew pictures of fighter jets on his creative assignments and wrote stories about Air Force heroes. Since our family actively discouraged any stories about warfare, we wondered where he had discovered these narrative threads. We prohibited our kids from owning toy guns, save for the ones that shot water, which we let them use with reservation. We were *those* kind of parents, trying hard to keep our values of peacemaking at the forefront, always.

And still, while visiting Vietnam on a return trip after his adoption ten years earlier, Benjamin insisted on a tour of the Cu Chi Tunnels, where Viet Cong soldiers hid during combat with the South Vietnam resistance and American forces. He expressed far more interest in Vietnam War sites than in the long-planned visit to the city of his birth and to places we thought significant to his heritage. In Hanoi, we drove by the lake where John McCain parachuted after his plane was downed, and Ben already knew the details of McCain's capture and his torture in Viet Cong prisons. He'd read about it sometime, and as we later toured the Hoa Lo prison, named the "Hanoi Hilton" by American prisoners of war, Ben recounted McCain's heroism as a Navy captain.

My husband, a Quaker by conviction, a man who had written several books about pacifism, found Benjamin's fascination perplexing—troubling even—and tried to provide abundant lessons on peacemaking. We could go to a military museum in Saigon, for sure, but Benjamin would need to learn the story of the My Lai Massacre too.

These educational attempts didn't appear to matter much. Our child was obsessed with the military, and nothing we could do could disabuse him, not books, not his Quaker Sunday school, not our frequent discourses on pacifism. For most families, this obsession might be lauded, an admiration for the military tightly woven into familial lore about a love of country and service and fighting for the American way. For my family, this obsession was far more complicated because my ancestral history includes a long line of Mennonite pacifists, conscientious objectors to war who believed that our Christian faith demands allegiance to only God, not country.

Benjamin graduated from high school in 2020. That year, he started meeting with military recruiters who had frequented the high school halls and who invited him to their nearby office, where he visited without our knowledge. His now-and-then talk about enlisting certainly had us worried, though he had also applied to several universities, including The Citadel, a military college in South Carolina. His acceptance there caused some parental angst, but then, in the summer of 2020, Ben decided to attend George Fox. We could rejoice, as Ben's dreams about the military seemed behind us.

Within a month of moving into the dorms, he'd found a girlfriend—this after disavowing girls and dating for much of his adolescence. We liked her, they seemed like a good match, and he talked about enjoying his coursework, even as he changed majors several times, even as we carefully avoided asking him directly about his grades, wanting him to find agency and independence in college.

One month before his first year at George Fox had ended, Benjamin let us know that he intended to enlist. He was nineteen then, and there was nothing we could do to stop him. But a week after the semester ended, the Army rejected him, his poor eyesight rendering him ineligible. We could breathe again, and imagined a future with him safely back at school. Apparently, the Navy played by separate rules, and several months later, after countless talks, cajoling and begging him to choose another path, Ben was gone, headed to boot camp and to a vocation in the Navy.

We said goodbye in a parking lot by the airport, and I cried all the way home.

For a long time, I assumed Benjamin's decision to enlist was fueled by the narrative of reckless courage. He was enthralled by YouTube videos of patriotic music swelling over battle scenes, created as recruitment tools by the US Armed Forces. Sometimes he showed the videos to my husband or to me, and what Ben saw as inspiration seemed to me propaganda intent on getting young people to commit years of their lives to a military effort. Pointing out our unease with what he was consuming could, at times, lead to good conversations with

Ben. More often than not, he responded with frustration, certain we could not understand what being in the military might mean for him. On this count, at least, he was right.

At some point during that summer's turmoil, a call with my niece helped me think differently about my son's decision to enlist. Katharina is one year younger than my sons, and lives in London, Ontario; she is a strong woman with strong convictions and a willingness to say what she means. Benjamin had expressed concerns about what his cousin, an ardent pacifist, would think when he enlisted. Yet she suggested to me that of all her cousins, Ben was the bravest one.

"We all do what's expected of us," Katharina said, by which she meant going to college, choosing a major, graduating in four years. "But Ben's actually doing what *he* wants to do, and doesn't care what other people think about it.

"I wish I could be as brave as him," she added.

Not one to be beholden to US military propaganda, Katharina was describing a different kind of courage—a willingness to follow his convictions, making a choice that challenged his family's expectations, pursuing his dream. Katharina wanted a similar strength, even if the decisions she made were different from her cousin's.

Once again, I realized, someone younger was teaching me to open my eyes, asking me to see.

About a decade ago, I coedited a book called *Just Moms*, a collection of essays from a variety of mothers trying hard to teach their children countercultural values: about peace and justice, avoiding materialism, advocating for gender and racial equity and for children with disabilities.[2] Working on that collection gave me hope and a sense of affinity. Other moms were facing the challenges I faced, putting prohibitions on gun play and first-person shooter games in the hopes of raising kids who would create a more just and peaceable world.

While I'm still proud of that book and the voices we gathered there, I'm also struck by how earnest the writers were, how hopeful and optimistic. Our kids were all much younger then, and we were still engaged in the difficult day-to-day work of parenting, using our considerable influence to teach the values that mattered most to us. I'm grateful that my kids learned about the central message of the Gospels to which we are called, about loving God and our neighbors. But I'm also less clear-eyed than I was back then, less certain that the values we hold dear will be automatically transmitted to our children if we just endeavor to do so. As my own kids grew into teenagers and then young adults, I became more aware that we cannot completely control the values our kids embrace. Benjamin's decision to enlist as a sailor initially made me doubt that my efforts mattered at all.

In this, I know I'm not alone. Staci and I started a friendship right when *Just Moms* came out, and I spoke at the church where she pastored about the book and its hope-filled premise. Like me, Staci has two sons, and like me, she ardently believed that the gender justice for which she advocated would be transmitted to her boys. As our kids grew, we had long conversations about the challenge of finding agency and affirmation in church traditions that often diminished women's voices. We talked about purity culture's corrosive impact on our own sexual ethic, and about our desire to provide our sons with a healthier view of sex and sexuality, of women and their worth.

Now that her eldest is in college she's second-guessed her approach, wondering and worrying whether everything she said and modeled has borne fruit in her kids. Staci wants her sons to be feminists, but she worries that the hookup culture so prevalent at many colleges undermines her message about respecting women for more than their bodies. She also worries that her son's sexual ethic is too facile. "I don't want him to treat sex so casually," she said. She wonders whether the baggage she's carried about purity culture from her own evangelical upbringing has somehow affected her reaction to what she describes as her son's hookups.

"Who's to say his approach to sex won't be damaging, or what is right or wrong?" she said. "It's really hard to not judge people who see sex as something you do like tying your shoes." Staci's self-awareness will no doubt help her as she navigates this challenge, although like most self-aware parents, she wonders what she got wrong, and whether it's even possible to transmit the values she holds dear in a way that doesn't heap shame on her sons' heads.

I know other parents have also had children take ideological paths far different from the ones they dreamed for them. Realizing that our young people are choosing different values can lead to a kind of loss, grief for what we hoped our children would become, for how closely they would embrace their parents' beliefs. We might also wonder what we've done wrong, regretfully recounting all the times we should have tried to reinforce our family's belief systems. I've wondered whether letting Benjamin play first-person shooter video games as a high schooler somehow affected his decision to enlist, or whether I should have insisted he attend Peace Camp at our church when he was twelve. Maybe that pressure would have been the impetus for a different life choice, one that kept him at a Quaker college studying conflict resolution.

Helping the children we love become adults means letting them choose their own value systems, no matter how much we hope to compel them to follow our footsteps exactly. From my own experience with my son, I'm here to say that this letting go can be wrenching, manifest in a summer's worth of pleading for Benjamin to accept our definition of peace-making and eschew the military. Whether we acknowledge it or not, letting go also requires a certain measure of humility: opening ourselves up to the uncertainty of who children will become, including when what they become is far different from what we imagined.

Our last meal with Benjamin before his boot camp departure was compromised by COVID protocols and the alarm of rising Delta infections. His favorite restaurant wasn't following masking and social distancing mandates, so we settled on a pizza shop near the airport where we could sit outside on a warm late-summer evening. His girlfriend was with us too. They'd driven to the airport separately from us, desperate for their last minutes together before he left. We were all desperate for time, knowing this goodbye would cause seismic changes in our relationships, our lives' tectonic plates shifting for good.

After dinner, we took pictures in a nearby park. The photos were reminiscent of images we'd taken when we met Ben nearly two decades earlier, something Ron and I noted on our tearful ride home: how much the tree cover and nearby traffic reminded us of the park in Saigon where we strolled with baby Benjamin. Given our emotional state and our longing to hold on to Ben's childhood, it could be that the two parks looked nothing alike at all.

We walked back to the parking lot after taking the photographs, and I felt my heart quicken, knowing this would be goodbye, that I would need to be brave in the face of this separation. Ben told us to wait, that he had something for me in his girlfriend's car. When he pulled out a box I recognized from his childhood birthday excursions to Build-A-Bear, I started sobbing. Ben pulled out the bear he'd made, dressed in military fatigues, and told me that when I pressed the bear's paw, I could hear a recording of Ben's voice saying "I love you, Mom." We hugged then, and said goodbye, and hugged some more. I didn't want to let go, but it was time.

Here's what you probably don't know, unless your child joins the military. Your child will phone you once they get to boot camp, a brief scripted call letting you know they have arrived safely. Training officers will be yelling at them when they call, and you will probably hear stress in your child's voice. Ben called my husband's phone, read the script, and when Ron said "We love you," Ben had already hung up. His script had ended, and there was no space to say more.

In the middle of some night, recruits are given sweats and T-shirts, measured for uniforms, assigned bunks. They put their civilian clothes and their cell phones in a box, which is stored until graduation. During boot camp, they might call from a pay phone every few weeks, or they might not. You can write old-fashioned letters, and they might write back. Or not. For the twelve weeks Ben was at boot camp, I heard his voice twice, in short phone calls. I pressed the bear's paw every day, and heard his voice then, too, all I really had to hold on to.

The first time our kids launch into the adult world might well be the hardest. People told me that each goodbye I had with my children after high school graduation would be difficult, but not as difficult as the one before. The goodbyes don't become completely pain-free, though, and especially for those whose kids move far away from home, the separation requires its own courage: a willingness to entrust our offspring to the capricious universe, to acknowledge we cannot control our children's futures. That control was always an illusion, at any rate, but having young adults leave home knocks that illusion off its already flimsy foundation.

Becoming a military mom that fall, I recognized the luxury of connection. Ben's life *was* an enigma; I had no sense what he was doing each day, no idea whether he was emotionally okay, no inkling of whether he regretted his decision to enlist or was thriving. He spent one month of training in the infirmary, misdiagnosed with asthma, and even then, we only knew that he was there, having no insight into why he was diagnosed or what that might mean for his future with the Navy. Only silence, and staying always close to the phone, just in case he had a chance to call.

Despite now having a son in the military, I am still a pacifist. Ardently so. I am grieved by the obscene budget of the US military industrial complex and detest our nation's fascination with violence. I read the Bible through a lens of nonresistance and believe that Jesus calls us to make peace, not war. Because of this, I especially despise attempts to reframe Scripture, to see in Jesus' life and death a justification for military might.

But my son is part of that military industrial complex now. Even though he's working in a noncombatant role, he knows how to use a gun, and he asserts that some wars are necessary to protect liberty. Benjamin also believes that God has called him to the Navy, and has seen every blockade removed—the Army's rejection, the medical waiver, the Navy's differing standards—as a sign that he is doing God's bidding.

In the months leading up to Benjamin's departure, I prayed often for understanding and acceptance. Ben's assurance that God had called him to the Navy was directly in conflict with my sense that God does not call us to make war, and I earnestly wanted to believe my son was following God's will. After all, I've spent my professional life at a Christian college helping young people think about and respond to God's vocational call, yet I wasn't willing to accept that perhaps Ben was doing exactly that: responding to the vocation to which he'd been called. Ben had processed his decision with his beloved youth pastor, a man of deep faith with a Quaker commitment to peacemaking. He'd talked with my parents, also lifelong pacifists. He'd prayed with family friends. His decision to join the Navy was not impetuous. Could I really tell my own son that he'd heard wrongly, and that every other adult in his life who was affirming this choice was wrong too? Or could I possibly possess the humility to trust that Benjamin's life is his own, and that his own choice to step aside from the values his parents embraced was also part of God's will?

Meeting another military mom in my home community became one way to process this tension between holding tightly to my deeply held convictions and supporting my son's calling to the Navy. Nancy has three sons, and her youngest is finishing his fifth year of Air Force service. She is also married to a Quaker pastor and understands well the challenges my family was facing. I met with her in the weeks before

Benjamin left for boot camp, and she shared her experience: about her son's enlistment, his deployment to the Middle East, and the conflict that emerged in her home between supporting her youngest son's vocation and her elder two sons' pacifism.

Her loving-kindness for her family managed to bridge the chasm developing between them, and I heard in her story a refrain that sustained me while Benjamin was at boot camp. I was reminded that the values guiding our children as they grow remain with them, even if they choose a different path. Our instruction still matters. Her son—and Benjamin— might be a light in the military, their peace-filled upbringing informing who they will become as airmen and sailors, and maybe God had called them to be this light.

Over the next months, as Ben embarked on his five-year enlistment, I returned to this prayer, *Let Ben be a light*, an incantation that helped form and reform me as well. I reminded my husband that Ben can be a light in the military, that our efforts might help him transform the very culture we cannot, because of our role as outsiders. *Let Ben be a light* continues to serve as a prayer that guides me, a hope-filled invocation that will continue to bear fruit, bolstered by the countless childhood lessons we gave Ben about making peace.

Praying for Benjamin to flourish in the military requires a fortitude I don't always possess, but if I want Ben to become who God created him to be, his flourishing is crucial.

My husband and I are unfamiliar with military culture, that much is clear. For most of my adult life, I've worn my outsider status as a weird badge of honor, proclaiming silently (well, mostly silently) that I am not like *those people*, the ones with American flags on their front lawns alongside signs saying "Support Our Troops." My Mennonite heritage has inoculated me from tearing up at patriotic hymns, or from cheering when the colors march by in a parade. I choose quiet cynicism instead, an internal eye roll at anyone who says "God bless America" on the Fourth of July or who affirms that freedom is never free and that soldiers sacrifice so we don't have to.

When that patriotic cant is tied to Christianity, my cynicism borders on rage—it is hard for me to fathom the Prince of Peace endorsing any violence, even for righteous causes. My PhD dissertation on Mennonite conscientious objectors in World War I only steeled my determination that the alchemy of patriotism and faith is toxic, as I read about my Anabaptist forebears facing physical abuse at the hands of fellow countrymen who carried a Bible in one hand and a sword in the other. The marriage of nationalism and Christianity, written into wartime propaganda, affirmed for me that I would never be able to support the military.

But there was my beautiful new friend Nancy, a Quaker pastor's wife for goodness' sake, inviting me into her home and telling me her story. She had an American flag on her front porch, a wreath made of camouflage fabric on her door, a picture of her son in full uniform on her wall. Nancy offered me tea from her vast collection, then told me that when her son joined the Air Force, she discovered an entire new community, one unceasingly hospitable to her and to her son. Other families with military connections had answered her early questions, calmed her anxieties, offered her son a place to rest when his truck broke down far away from base. Though all these families were strangers, their open-heartedness had opened Nancy's heart—and I would soon discover, was beginning to open mine.

Shortly after Benjamin left for boot camp, I joined several Facebook groups for the families of Navy recruits, including other families whose sons and daughters had joined the same division that Ben had. Even though I'd mostly sworn off Facebook, these people became a lifeline for me, a connection to my son forged through a connection to others who were also missing their loved ones. Their kindness sustained me during the lonely weeks when I had only a Build-A-Bear's paw giving me access to my son's voice. The month that Benjamin was waylaid in the infirmary, other mothers answered questions and shared their own frustrations with the Navy's "hurry up and wait" culture, where sailor recruits find themselves rushed through enlistment, then entangled by bureaucratic paperwork. They introduced outsiders like me to naval traditions, helped us understand the perplexing array of acronyms, and explained what my son was probably experiencing at each point of boot camp.

The Facebook community provided a great space to commiserate, and I found myself opening up to strangers, telling them how much I missed my son, receiving a virtual BNH (that is, a Big Navy Hug). Just months earlier, I might have been cynical about BNHs, but here I was, my need for solidarity and comfort wearing the edges off my cynicism and allowing me to see the true nature of my bigotry, my self-assurance of righteousness about my pacifism challenged by the loving-kindness of strangers.

In my letters to Ben, I told him about the Facebook group, how it allowed me insight into a culture that had been mostly foreign to me. I apologized for the grief I'd caused him over the summer, when I'd said some words intended to express my enduring love for him, my concern for his well-being, but which he heard as condemnation and control. The few times that Ben wrote me back, I could hear in his letters a shift occurring for him too. Always a child who thought deeply, Benjamín was processing his boot camp experience in profound ways. He seemed to be maturing, finding some of the grounding and focus he'd struggled to discover during high school. I wondered whether, perhaps, he was becoming the light in the military, for which I continue to pray.

It's true that Ben's enlistment was seismic for our family, but perhaps the ground shifting under us was what we needed—what I needed—to recognize what walking humbly with God might look like: being proud of a son whose deeply held convictions challenge my deeply held biases, compelling me to change. And then, having the humility to be transformed.

Despite the past year's challenges, Benjamin's decision to enlist has not tempered our love for him, nor our admiration for his courage and his steadfastness, even if those character traits have led him down a pathway of beliefs far different from our own. At times, I still wonder whether there will be shifts in my sons' value systems or choices that I wouldn't countenance, causing estrangement: *What if one of my sons becomes a white supremacist or misogynist or a far-right provocateur?* Some parents seemed to definitively claim that their ideologies matter more than their children: I think especially of the LGBTQIA people disowned by parents whose certainty about God's will means abandoning their queer children to navigate life without their first families.

I've witnessed models of humility that seem like a better choice. Nancy, my Quaker-and-military-mom mentor, expressed humility when talking about what might lead to estrangement in her family. She considered what she might do if one of her sons became stuck in racist or misogynistic ideologies. "My empathy would be so strong," she said, "that I couldn't imagine my sons doing something awful without wondering what the underlying reasons are for their actions." Instead of pursuing estrangement, Nancy said she would seek to understand what happened to them, and would try to help them work through why they were rejecting what she sees as the fundamental message of the Gospels: "To love God, and to love others."

Young adults intent on finding their way in relationship with parents and mentors recognize that there's also humility in loving parents who disagree with them. Hannah L., who is a queer Christian, grew up in a conservative evangelical family and was homeschooled with her siblings. In her last years of high school, she struggled with mental illness and suicidal ideation, and arrived at college still clinging to her parents' faith. In time, as she got healthier, she recognized her identity as a queer Christian, and by her senior year was leading a chapel worship band, the first openly gay person on our campus who fulfilled that role—and did so brilliantly. Her parents haven't always done or said the right thing about Hannah's transformation, as they are still seeped in their conservative faith. She realized that she "doesn't need Christian fundamentalism to be valued," and she wishes her dad "wouldn't freak out so much" about the changes she's made in her life.

In the past few years, though, Hannah's parents have shifted too, not holding so tightly to their sense that Hannah needs to renounce being queer if she wants to know God. They are letting Hannah become who God created her to be. "My parents see the light in me," Hannah said, "even if they don't agree with me." Hannah said that when her mom says something inelegant about her life and queer identity, "I'm able to translate what she says, knowing that she is responding out of love. My mom sees me and knows my heart, in the same way that I see and know my mom's heart."

This is humility exemplified.

This is a family's longing to see each other, rather than see past each other.

This is a shining light.

Of course, our mentoring and love for young adults does not end when they walk out the door, and conflicts over value systems will no doubt linger far into adulthood. In our polarized culture, it seems like those differences can cut even deeper, creating large chasms in families, separating parents from children. How can those divides even be bridged, save for a recognition that we are all created in the very image of God; and the courage to accept that different ideologies do not abrogate the *imago Dei*; and the empathy to acknowledge that aberrant ideologies bloom in broken hearts, and that we are called to do the mending?

When I was writing this chapter, the conflict in Ukraine festered into a bloody war, and my son's decision to join the military took on a different hue. I told myself and others that if Ben made it to the front lines, the world would be in deep trouble, given how new he was to the Navy, and given how many other soldiers and sailors would have to perish before he, a culinary specialist, might be ordered to fight.

Even after he was deployed to an aircraft carrier meant to support NATO, I reminded myself and others that Ben was probably safe. But the needless war, the tragedy of it all, has been a reminder of how abhorrent violence really is, and how much the Prince of Peace must grieve for the loss and destruction. The news from Ukraine made me think most of the Russian and Ukrainian mothers whose sons and daughters were senselessly asked to fight a war not of their making, and of how many have buried children who were their entire world, just as my sons are mine. My mind turned to the leaders who have made decisions that destroy so many lives, and I wonder how the *imago Dei* has been distorted in them by power, and money, and the ability to decimate cities with one spoken order.

And of course, I thought of my son, deciding to join the military when his parents wanted him to do almost anything but. I hope to someday have the courage of his convictions, but I also hope the world he and his brother create will not be one where violence is endemic.

Letting go of the expectations for our children takes extravagant courage because it means relinquishing control to what seems an impetuous universe, where powerful leaders can drop bombs on civilians and live in luxury while others starve. We are forced to decide: Will we live by the illusion that we can protect our children, and ourselves, from the vagaries of a threatening world or will we respond with faith that God's love is ascendent despite what threatens, even when our young adults choose values that differ from our own?

Walking humbly with God requires embracing an impulse of faith, choosing an open-hearted acceptance of others even when that could mean relinquishing our visions about what lifelong relationships with young people might look like. For one mother I know, this humility has meant accepting that her son will contact her only a few times each year. The distance hurts, she said, but she's resigned herself to this limited connection, knowing she did her best to raise him. Several mothers acknowledged that their longing to become grandparents will most likely not come true because their offspring are choosing to be child-free. I expressed sadness to one mom, and she said, "What else am I going to do? I pray a lot that God will help me accept my kids for who they are, and that I can let go."

Sometimes, releasing such expectation is the most loving act we can do, one that requires considerable humility and considerable faith.

We flew to Chicago in early December for Ben's boot camp graduation, one month later than planned because of the misdiagnosed asthma that kept Ben from training. In early September before Ben left, my husband had expressed dismay about attending the graduation, insisting that Ben's girlfriend should get one of the two tickets allotted for the ceremony. By late fall, Ron had started to shift, too, and decided he really wanted to see Ben graduate after all. Kelcie still came with us and would watch the graduation via livestream from our hotel. After the ceremony, Ben had been given a few hours of liberty to see all of us before he transferred to another base for continued training.

In the air somewhere over Idaho, we had each received phone messages from Ben telling us he'd officially passed all his tests and would be graduating. This is the "I'm a sailor!" call that families anticipate in the last week of boot camp, when recruits complete physical tests and something called Battle Stations, a twelve-hour ship simulation that challenges them to recall the skills they've learned. The phone messages were long, and I could hear in Ben's exhausted voice a confidence I'd not witnessed before. Years earlier, he'd earned a second-degree black belt in tae kwon do, but that achievement seemed to pale when juxtaposed with the trials he faced and overcame at boot camp. I only wished I could have taken that call in person.

Placed awkwardly in my carry-on bag was a wooden anchor decorated in navy blue and with Ben's name, his graduation date, and his division number painted on it. I had reached out to several crafters in my community to help me make this, a decoration that Navy families put on their hotel room doors the night before graduation, another ritual I learned from my Facebook group that I might have sneered at only months earlier. As we deplaned at O'Hare, I notice another mom carrying a wooden anchor, and I asked her about her child, a daughter it turned out, who'd be graduating too. *Who even am I?* I wondered after the conversation ended, grateful for the random connection.

The next morning, we arrived on base at six thirty, having been warned by other parents to get there early. The large viewing hall was already filling with families, so we found a sign for Ben's division and parked ourselves on bleachers in front of it, hoping for a better view of our son. For two hours we waited, watching as a big screen displayed videos about America's military might, patriotic songs, and images of what kind of training occurred at the Great Lakes Naval Base.

When the battalions marched into the viewing stadium, we couldn't find our son: every uniform looked the same, and because of COVID, the sailors were wearing masks. For two hours more, we watched as the sailors did formations, stood at attention, chanted the Navy oath. Every now and again, when the patriotic rhetoric intensified, I'd glance at my husband and wonder what in the world we were doing there, in this entirely new world.

Finally, after twelve weeks, it was time to hug our son. Finding him in the scrum of military uniforms and parents was difficult, but then he was there, the same kid I've loved intensely for twenty years, who also seemed completely different. We hugged, and neither of us really wanted to let go. I was so proud of him and the courage he exhibited in discovering who God created him to be.

My son Benjamin Quan may have had warrior written into his name. But I also see who he is becoming. On those days when I want to hold on tight to the boy I raised, I pray for Ben's light, and for the humility to let go so he can shine.

SHORT EXERCISES

1. How have the young adults in your life surprised you by
their differing values? Have young adults compelled you to
rethink your values and where those values come from?
Reflect on these questions, then consider reaching out to a
young person and sharing the ways that person has challenged you to rethink what you value.

2. What would happen if the young adults you love chose a
different set of values from the ones you believe central to
your being? Is there anything that might be a deal breaker
for you? How could you express empathy for their decision
to embrace another set of values?

3. In what ways are your young adults choosing to be a light in
their contexts? Consider sending them a letter, a text, or an
email that affirms that light in them.

SIX

To Loving Mercy

Graduation happens twice a year at my university, an event I approach with equal parts dread and thanksgiving. The long speeches might be boring, but we've made it to another semester's end, hallelujah and amen. I still get caught up in the pageantry of the moment, the chance to wear my doctoral robes, to feel regal in a *Pomp and Circumstance* processional. Never mind that I generally have a handful of Runts in my pocket, my snack for the ceremonies; the humor is not lost on me, Ms. PhD eating fake banana candy in her fine black robes.

After the too-long speeches are finished, my sugar high crashes. As the conferring of diplomas drags on, I cheer for departmental graduates crossing the stage, then slide into an inertia that lasts until the recessional. The robes are hot, and puffy, the faculty seats so close that we seem to be wearing not only our own robes, but the ones on either side of us too.

By the time the benediction is said, all pretense of majesty is behind me, and I'm ready to slide off my robe, finish my candy, and head into the winter or summer break.

What stands between me and that freedom is saying goodbye to graduating students, the young people I've grown to love during our time together at the university. I hate this moment of farewell, the final hugs that signal a parting, a shift in our relationship from *in loco parentis* to something else entirely: I become a peer, a writer of recommendations, an old professor to visit during homecoming weekends. Every graduation is difficult because of how much I love these young people. Some years, it is excruciating.

The recessional usually deposits us all into the quad, and if it's not raining, families linger there for photographs. There's an implicit expectation that faculty will mingle too, before hanging robes in our office closets and heading for the hills. The party unfolding in the quad is a happy affirmation of the work we do at the university, but I'm not much of a mingler, especially not now, not when I'm on the verge of tears because I have to say goodbye to people who have become like friends.

I hug all of them in my big billowy robes, save for the ones who prefer a high-five. And over their shoulders, just beyond the graduates, I see their families, the parents' pride so obvious, it nearly crushes me. I'm reminded again how much these young people are cherished, how much of their lives exist beyond the walls of my classroom. I struggle to know exactly what to say to families, how I can articulate the wonder of knowing their children. My attempts often seem cliched, hollow: *It's been a pleasure to work with your son*, I might say, or *Your child is fabulous. She will go far!*

Because I teach writing classes, and because writing can be so personal, I often know more about these families than they realize. The confessional nature of students' work means I find out intricate details about their lives, including their most painful moments. I also learn about parents' mistakes, how words spoken when their child was younger reverberate, the parents' actions years earlier shaping how their children see the world now. A mom critical of her teenager's fashion choices compels the daughter to second-guess every piece of jewelry she wears. A dad pushing his kids to academic success fills another student with anxiety and grief. Parents demand their family attend a church whose theology erases the child's dreams, making their daughter choose a major she despises: she wants to preach, but her faith tradition says being a nurse or a teacher is a more acceptable vocation for women. I read these essays, and even then my responses to students seem hollow. How can I quantify their most painful moments up to this point in their lives by giving them a letter grade? Assessment proves difficult—impossible—because their writing offers the chance for me to encounter beauty and tragedy and humanity again and again.

When I was younger, when my kids were much younger, I often felt righteous indignation for the students as I read their essays, for what they had suffered by their parents' transgressions. How could these parents be so daft, I thought, so willing to put their emotional needs and their desire for control above their kids' longing for agency and self-expression? At the time, I didn't realize my own capacity to make mistakes that mattered, to say the wrong thing that cut deeply, to regret the moment my anger made me lash out or my selfishness drove me to think carelessly about my sons' feelings.

Now that my kids have passed through their teens, though, compassion floods me as I see graduates and their families standing there smiling, a tidal wave of love and pride washing over the parents. Of course, some families' dysfunction feels beyond the pale, and when I read stories about abuse, rejection, cold disregard for others, my compassion is limited, my ability to warmly greet those parents complicated by what I know. Usually, though, my students' writing is a mirror, a reflection of my best and worst tendencies as a parent, because I am also human, because I too have made mistakes. And so when I hug the new graduates, express how proud I am, I long to reach beyond them, to embrace the people standing behind them, these folks who have often tried their best, and just as often—like me—faltered in their imperfect love for others.

On days like this, when we observe academic achievement with *Pomp and Circumstance* and black robes and a little bit of candy, we are also celebrating the loving mercy of our flawed best selves. And God rejoices.

Dear Lord, *I have made mistakes.*

I say this as an invocation and a confession, an admission of my failures, and a prayer that God and my children and my students will treat me with loving mercy, despite my faults, my blind spots, my inability to love perfectly with the flawless ease I see in so many others. Who, let's face it, have probably made ample mistakes too.

At times, when I'm filled with regret about my transgressions, my body aches with a metaphysical longing to go back in time, to make things right by doing the right thing. I cannot fully enumerate the number of times I reacted with anger rather than empathy. It was so much easier to ask my kids to forgive me when they were younger, and my offenses less profound. Apologizing for getting the wrong cereal or showing up to their soccer game a few minutes late was easy, and my sons were consistently willing to extend forgiveness: there was still cereal to eat, a soccer game to play. When I've apologized for recent mistakes, like making assumptions about their actions that proved untrue or pointing out a character flaw I told them to fix, I've recognized that grace is not cheap, and that my sons are extending extravagant mercy to me, a loving-kindness that feels unwarranted.

This is the very definition of loving mercy. My sons don't owe me any grace, yet they offer it, and in abundance. When I grapple with what the exhortation to love mercy in Micah 6:8 really means, I need only recall the countless times I've knocked on my sons' slammed bedroom doors, asking for entry, needing to make right a situation that my words made wrong. I'm aware that their willingness to let me in, over and over again, so I can sit on their beds and apologize, is its own manifestation of mercy. They aren't required to forgive me because I'm older, or wiser, or because I fed and clothed them for the past twenty years. (More emphatically: my sons owe me nothing for my having adopted them, and the insistence that adoptees owe a debt to their parents is anathema to the idea of family.) Yet they do, forgive me that is, by this point seventy times seven and more.

And the brave students who knock on my office door? Who admit that an exchange in class hurt their feelings? Who want to talk about a reading assignment that aggravates their tender hearts? They, too, are teaching me loving mercy. Just today, a journalism student reached out, wanting to meet.

Sheryl was breathless when she reached my office—the steep stairs in the building have that effect on people—and jittery, nervous about what she'd decided to say: that she felt unfairly targeted in my class as a conservative because my assigned readings too often criticized right-wing media outlets. With considerable courage, she called out my biases, asking me to see and know her. We talked about the difficulty of studying journalism in an era of alternative facts, and about how disinformation has destroyed our trust in institutions and each other. I explained why I'd selected the course reading, and apologized for the angst I'd caused; I promised to try to be more thoughtful in my curriculum choices. Sheryl and I might never agree about what I see as the threats to our democracy, but I will be a better human because of our conversation, and because of her willingness to extend grace to a flawed professor, a gift she may never realize she's given me.

When we think about parent and child relationships—or a professor and student relationship—we often assume that those with power (the parent, the professor) will need to extend forgiveness to young adults, whose undeveloped frontal lobes mean they will continue to make mistakes deserving our grace. We use terms like "childhood indiscretions" to suggest that young people will be impulsive, careless, prone to stumbling over life's obstacles and in need of our consistent, unfailing grace. I've worked with young adults long enough to know that those indiscretions exist, and that we are given the opportunity to shower our young people with the abundant loving mercy they need.

But many times it's the older adults to whom grace should be extended. Mary, whose daughter is thirty-six, provided a succinct mantra to live by in this regard. "Don't apologize *for* your children," Mary said, "but apologize *to* your children." She noted that acknowledging our mistakes to our children, and asking for grace, models respect and love to them. Because I know Mary as a grace-filled woman who exudes love, I trust that she lives this out every day with her only child, someone who has experienced significant barriers to thriving. Mary didn't always practice what she preaches, she said, but when she stopped judging her daughter and started following the tenets of her faith as a Baha'i, she found that unconditional love and a lack of judgment for her daughter's choices were transformative: for her daughter, and for herself as well.

I want to follow Mary's example in this regard. Like Mary, I want to acknowledge the countless mistakes I make because I am fallible, because although I want badly to be a perfect mom and teacher, I often fail. The transitional moment we're in as parents and mentors presents a remarkable opportunity to be receptors of mercy from young people, who are now developmentally at the age when they start to recognize that the adults in their lives are humans too. Abigail, twenty-three, offered me a compelling explanation for this, saying that "becoming independent helped me realize the deep wounds of my parents, and how I've been wounded by them." She credited the geographical distance from them, as well as individuation, for helping her consider her parents in a new light.

Another young adult showed extraordinary empathy for her parents and the journey they have taken in dealing with her queerness. She'd seen how some of her peers were treated by families once they came out—so many in her own circles faced alienation from parents unable to extend compassion. Becca had seen the fallout from parental estrangement, her friends left alone and lonely because their parents chose rigid ideology over relationship with their queer children.

"I get it," Becca said. "They are afraid that their children are going to hell, which is the worst fate possible. Because they are acting out of fear, what they do makes more sense." By God's grace, this former student and her parents have done the hard work of trying to see each other rather than past each other. In the six years I've known her, I've watched as her relationship with her parents shifted. They've become more accepting of their daughter, more willing to listen to her story. She's become more willing to understand the challenges they've faced and continue to face in changing their perspective about queerness and what that means for their child. Their longing to fully know each other, and to know empathy's power, has made this possible.

Even in our angry and painful moments, even when it's far easier to lash out and impugn the young people we love most in the world, we need to be safe harbors for them. Finding our way forward might mean seeking to understand the nature of grace, the power of God's loving mercy for us, and our loving mercy for each other. Self-aware parents know they aren't always the safe harbors they want to be and can acknowledge that loving mercy is often aspirational. We sometimes make unfounded assumptions about the young adults we love, complicating our relationships. One former student, Marci, twenty-three, told me one of the biggest challenges she's faced with her parents is their tendency to interpret her actions in a negative light, to make assumptions about her choices without checking in with her or asking her to explain herself. Because of their own upbringing, their unmoored young adulthood, and the choices they made before finding faith and stability, her parents are inclined to project ill intentions on Marci and her siblings. This feels to Marci like a lack of loving mercy, a dehumanization that makes her only a repository of her parents' worst assumptions rather than someone striving to be the woman God is creating her to be.

While Marci and I talked, I recognized myself not in Marci or her grief, but in her parents' lack of charity and my easy propensity to interpret young adults' behavior in a negative light, making little space for empathy. In my professional life especially, I've drawn conclusions about students' behavior, judging their truancy as apathy and assuming that students who fail to complete assignments are lazy or undisciplined, or deciding that the young men who slump in desks with ball caps pulled low over their eyes are more interested in sports than in whatever my classes have to offer. Each year, I'm reminded to check myself, with my failure to think kindly of my students brought up short by an email from them explaining a family crisis, or by a long talk in my office about their challenges, or by an essay they've written showing a deep well of creativity I'd not acknowledged.

I'm sure most of us can catalog instances where mercy was lacking in our response to young people, including those we love most. When against our advisement one of our sons made the choice to quit a barista job after working there only a few weeks, my first response was anger: quitting a good paying job without prospects for another was not something we did in our family. I was embarrassed when the other son joked about smoking weed and bought a novelty shirt festooned with a marijuana leaf pattern. Using such substances is not condoned in my family, and I couldn't fathom why my son was posing as a pothead. My lack of charity for their situations and my unwillingness to meet their choices with empathy caused damage to our relationships because I made assumptions about their motivations, writing narratives in my head that had little to do with the reality of their situations. In those moments, they didn't need more judgment from me. What they required was an open-hearted desire to understand why one felt compelled to quit a job he needed, and why the other believed pot, or even the illusion of smoking pot, would blunt his emotional pain.

One of my former students, Alice, twenty-four, helped me think with clarity about the uncharitable narratives we are tempted to write about the young adults we love. I watched Alice grow up with her three siblings, as I knew her parents socially. They seemed the image of the perfect Christian family, with a stay-at-home mom who homeschooled and who, I was sure, judged me silently for continuing to work outside the home when my boys were young. The mother especially wanted to foster a perfect childhood for her family and worked hard to cultivate nurturing experiences. Now grown up, the young adults have faced challenges, including a sibling's gender transition. Alice's conservative parents struggled with this, especially her mom. In the early years after Alice's sibling came out as queer, the parents gathered with church members to pray that their child might renounce their queer "lifestyle," but over the past decade, the parents have realized that transitioning might be exactly what Alice's sibling needs to become who God created them to be.

"My mom said that she'd been writing her daughter's narrative for her entire life," Alice said. That narrative did not include a gender transition, queerness, challenges with mental health. "She finally realized that Jamie's narrative was not [the mom's] to write, and that Jamie needed to write her own life story, whatever that might be."

We spend our children's first few decades crafting stories about who they will become, stories forged by our dreams and expectations. We imagine the future we hope for them. Young adults have also spent their formative years cultivating a persona, shaped by who they assume their families and peers want them to be, and by their own deep longings to be relevant and loved in a world that can feel hostile and unforgiving. But as Alice's mom affirmed, our children's narratives are not ours to write, nor can they be written by cultural mythologies or the demands of an unpredictable universe that tells them who they are supposed to be.

Mercy is allowing our children to craft their own life stories, ones that bear witness to their fearful, wonderful, unique selves. Mercy is refusing to make assumptions about the stories they are writing. Mercy is listening to their stories with open hearts and minds. And mercy means letting them make mistakes as they figure out who they are. Because they will make mistakes, and we will too.

For the span of years when my sons were really struggling, I told very few people about the challenges we were facing, not even my parents; I didn't want my mom and dad to think badly of my children, or of me. Many parents navigating similar difficulties with their kids also choose silence, well aware of the judgment that rains down on those who don't follow the road map outlined by cultural expectations. In a social media environment where oversharing has become the norm, people are far less likely to admit when their families are fraying at the edges, and thus less likely to get the support they need to weather particular storms. Forget our aspirations to be perfect. Most of us just want to be seen as competent, good parents and mentors, and we know that when our kids aren't seen as good, by whatever means that term is defined, then neither are we.

We may need to recognize that our cultural definition of what makes someone good is problematic, premised on a belief that some people are more valuable than others simply by virtue of their social class, their race and ethnicity, their adherence to faith, even the way they look or think. Let's face it: we all have internalized scripts telling us what a good family is, or what good people look like. We even have a phrase to codify that notion: *They're good people.* My son Ben was considered a *good baby* from the moment we brought him home because he didn't cry except when he was hungry. The reason he rarely cried had little to do with my competent parenting— rather, he learned in his first months that crying yielded little change in his circumstances, his being in an orphanage and all. Yet when children enter the world we've already decided that good babies are ones who don't cry, aren't too demanding, are compliant to their parents' wishes. Who decided that this makes a baby good? Who makes decisions about what defines a good adult, or good parents?

If we truly are people of the Word, we might do well to see what Scripture says about goodness, and about what being good looks like. In the Gospels, Jesus tells a multitude of stories that upend definitions about who has value, and even Jesus' birth suggests that worth is determined not by the accoutrements of wealth and royalty, but by humility, as demonstrated by his birth in a stable amid lowly animals.

Story after story in the Gospels reminds Jesus' followers that it's not the rich and powerful who inherit the kingdom, but the meek and marginalized: A poor woman overturning her house, looking for a lost coin. The Samaritan, reviled by his community, who extends roadside care. A beggar at the gates, asking for water. A woman accused of adultery, and another afflicted with bleeding, whom Jesus heals. The Gospels challenge us to reconsider our assumptions about who matters in our communities, and also to reform what we mean when we call someone good.

Loving mercy demands that we recognize that our fundamental goodness is not derived from anything we can do, and then acting on that knowledge. We are good just because we exist, inherently worthy because of our creation as an image of our Creator. This is true of the young people we love, even those who seem entirely separated from God, from their families, from any sense of morality. If we could, like Jesus, reform our understanding of goodness and worth, perhaps that might change how we relate to young adults, seeing their challenges with a heart of empathy, responding with mercy rather than condemnation, and giving them the support they need to live happy, whole, and holy lives. That support shouldn't mean we coddle them, giving young adults everything they ask for and refusing to hold them accountable for their choices. It is possible to hold these impulses in tension, though, making sure that we also walk alongside them, extending the grace needed to comprehend their struggles, then helping them find their way to a more settled life apart from our own.

This loving mercy might mean recognizing the ways young adults have been traumatized, wounded, broken by the generational horrors they've experienced. This might mean connecting them to resources that can help them heal. This might mean offering grace to ourselves, to our own limitations, our own trauma and wounds, and this might mean working on ourselves rather than trying to fix everyone around us. We should make these efforts not because doing so will make us look more virtuous or better. We should make these efforts because we are all inherently worthy of mercy, no matter who we are. We are all inherently good, no matter what we do. Our primary identity is not in our goodness, but because we are beloved.

"Kindness is about empowerment," Hannah L. told me, with a confidence and transparency I've long appreciated in her, even when she was a much younger student in my journalism class. Hannah works as a Starbucks barista. Like other young adults, she's been a lightning rod for workplace anger. We've all read the stories cataloging violent outbursts in restaurants and coffee shops as people explode at cashiers and baristas because their orders aren't right. Young adults like Hannah face these stressors often, if only because many people her age populate service industry jobs. A shortage of workers, alongside supply chain issues, has stretched people in these jobs, making it harder to deliver the same standard of service. "It costs zero dollars to be kind," Hannah said. Yet she hates her job in large part because people are exceedingly unkind, making demands and throwing fits over things she cannot control. She feels that each shift is a risk, her emotional and physical well-being jeopardized by people seeking overpriced coffee drinks and reacting poorly when their demands are not perfectly met.

Hannah's second job is as a peer tutor in the university's Academic Resource Center, a place where her clients—fellow students, mostly—are far kinder to the employees. Her encounters with students have allowed her to note the vast difference between those demanding a pumpkin latte at Starbucks and a peer seeking help to succeed in his classes. It is easy to extend kindness to students, Hannah said, because she knows she is also empowering them, a reciprocal relationship that turns on the fundamental nature of mercy and of extending empathy to others.

Meeting with a student struggling to succeed in his classes, Hannah didn't immediately offer study pointers or help him set up a calendar. Instead, she listened to his concerns and empathized with his fears of failure because she's had those fears too. Someone (like, say, even me) might assume the student was lazy or unmotivated, his poor grades a reflection of how little he cared about college. By simply listening to him, letting him tell his story, Hannah helped him think with more clarity, empowering him to speak with professors and get the reasonable assistance he needed to succeed.

The fix seems so obvious in this situation, yet Hannah reminded me that it is rare for young adults to feel truly seen by the grownups around them. In her work with the Academic Resource Center, she has unique insight into the academic challenges faced by her peers and noted that professors sometimes show little grace for students who are struggling. "COVID has us second-guessing everything," she said, and when professors set down draconian principles and offer little flexibility for the very real humans in their midst, their lack of mercy can be devastating.

"We are all kind of lost," Hannah added, "and we need kind people to affirm the decisions we are making." According to Hannah, the most substantial gift we can offer is to empower young adults by empathizing with their experiences, rather than assigning negative motives to their every act. Doing so takes patient effort and a willingness to listen without making assumptions. These are character virtues in short supply right now, creating a fecund environment for hostility and anger and unkindness to bloom.

What young adults need, what we all need, is a different world entirely, one built with loving mercy, grace, and the patience to find out who people are and who they are created to be. The Gospels provide us a good blueprint for this work. There, Jesus extended mercy to those who might be considered his enemies, even in his crucifixion asking that God forgive those who killed him. The best-known stories in the Gospels reflect Jesus' mercy: the woman at the well, the feeding of five thousand, his healing of the leper, his visit with Zacchaeus. Over and over, Jesus expressed compassion for those he met, a longing to understanding who they were in all their complexity, alongside his call for justice and his humble obedience to God. If we're ever at a loss for what loving mercy looks like and how we can extent kindness to the young people we love, we need only turn to the Gospels and to the model Jesus provided there.

Hannah ended our conversation by saying that "empathetic conversations are crucial, the only real way to find peace." I thought again about the disagreements roiling our communities. About the lack of empathetic conversations, and the way that people malign those who are suffering. About the arguments that unspool on social media and are carried into our churches and homes, separating families and friends from each other. I thought about students like Hannah and the ways their empathy has made a difference for so many others. About my sons, who have patiently listened to my apologies a thousand times over, extending me undeserved grace. About how these young people's compassion has transformed the lives of their peers; their grace has changed me too.

We all have work to do to extend mercy, and the Gospels provide us a road map to follow. Finding our way forward with young adults through empathy might not always be easy, but empathy is what all of us need more of right now.

SHORT EXERCISES

1. Write an apology letter to one of the young adults you love about a current conflict or an unresolved conflict from your past. Acknowledge the ways you may have hurt this person, and ask for forgiveness. What would it take for you to address the content of this letter with this person? What's holding you back from doing so?

2. Given the often angry and divisive environment in which we're living, where can you make space in your life for mercy? Write about one specific way you can extend mercy, and then follow through with this real, tangible act.

3. Make a list of the people who have expressed mercy to the young people you love: one of their friends, a teacher or manager, a pastor. Write a thank you note to that person for the kindness they've extended. Receiving such affirmations can sometimes be transformative, can remind us that our acts of kindness are seen and appreciated.

SEVEN

To a Deeper Faith

For twenty years, my family served as balcony dwellers at our Quaker church: even though the wooden pews creaked each time we moved, even though I got a little woozy by the heights when we stood for singing, even though most of the congregation sat in the padded seats below and we were a little detached, way up near the eaves. I liked the smattering of folks sitting near us, our own little community of latecomers and introverts who made haste during the greeting time to say hello before retreating to our self-assigned seats. My family sat to the pastor's left, in the second balcony row, and on rare occasions when someone arrived before us, unwittingly taking our spot, we stood at the doorway, stunned by the audacity. We were those people. We were that comfortable.

A smattering of young adults sat near us for several years, people on the verge of graduating high school or just after. Some were students in my college classes; some, my friends' kids, now out on their own but still tied to their home congregation. I loved watching them interact, admired the friendships they'd fostered over years of attending Sunday school and youth group and summer camp. When my sons were younger, it was easy to imagine them sitting with a similar crowd someday, their shared upbringing keeping them connected to the church, to each other, and so to us.

About a decade ago, our congregation started to crumble, increasingly divided—like so many other churches—by the question of full inclusion for LGBTQIA people, including some of those young adults sitting near us in the balcony. Attempts by leadership to hold the church together despite deep divisions couldn't stem the breaking. My family kept coming to church each week, and the group of young people were still there, faithfully, even though they felt the ground shifting underneath them. They had to wonder, too, whether the foundation had been so firm in the first place.

By 2016, the idea of a church split was inching closer to reality. Congregational surveys about inclusion showed a deep chasm separating two camps, with few people in the middle. The pastoral team held listening sessions, hoping the two sides might find a bridge to each other, and at first, those young people attended, still faithful to the church and its people, the ones who had raised them to cherish the Quaker values of consensus, of equity and justice, of seeing that of Christ in everyone. At those meetings, some older congregants, including ones who had served as wise mentors, Sunday school teachers, and camp counselors, denounced what they believed the grave sin of homosexuality. Their index fingers jabbed at open Bibles, angrily pointing to scripture texts they were certain proved their cause.

An abomination, they said. A violation of God's will, a stain on our church.

But we love you, of course, they added.

One person described the sessions as like being in an abusive relationship, pummeled with invectives by the same people who insist that they are acting in love, that the verbal assaults about wickedness and evil are only for the instruction of those being battered. Yet the young adults kept coming back, asking for respect, for a hearing. Their elders had taught them Quaker theology well, and they were convicted that God was leading them to speak truth.

They kept coming back, until they didn't. By 2017, our church was so deeply divided that despite a summer spent in mediation, the only reasonable solution seemed to be a split. The predominantly older congregants kept the church building but hemorrhaged members and the entire church leadership team, who could no longer countenance a faith that described humans, created in God's image, as a stain on the fellowship of believers. Those young adults I'd watched in the balcony also scattered, rightly wounded by a congregation who had nurtured them into adulthood, reminded them continuously about God's goodness and unconditional love, and then suggested their very lives were a disgrace, not worthy of inclusion: either because they were gay or because they loved their gay friends.

For many, their ties to any church severed completely. Young adults couldn't imagine God would look like an angry man standing in the pews, shaking a Bible and calling them wicked. The God they knew and loved—the God of mercy and justice—could be found in other places. They didn't need an institution insisting there is really only one way to love God.

Recent statistics suggest that today's young people are far more invested in social justice than their parents' generation is. They were teenagers during the racial upheaval ignited by the killing of Michael Brown in Ferguson and the vigilante murder of Trayvon Martin, and in 2020, many were motivated to participate in protests after Derek Chauvin kneeled on George Floyd's neck for over nine minutes. According to several surveys, they are far more open than elders when it comes to gender and sexual identity, and detached from the weight of shame their parents felt, they are more willing to experiment with their own identities. Young adults have also been witnesses to climate catastrophes that expose a burning planet, and are more engaged in efforts to stop accelerating environmental disasters brought on by climate change.

It's not difficult to imagine a connection between their interest in social justice and a departure from organized religion. They are preferring to "live out their values," *Religion Dispatches* reported in November 2021, rather than participate in faith communities. The same article notes that in a survey of ten thousand young people by Springtide Research Institute, a majority of young people (71 percent) said they are at least "slightly religious," though few (16 percent) saw their faith communities as places to turn to when they experience challenges in their lives.[1] Those surveyed are part of a growing population of "nones" (that is, people who express no religious affiliation) and "dones" (people who express religious belief but are no longer actively involved in an organized religious institution, like a church). So many members of Gen Z and beyond express this detachment from their faith communities that one researcher has called this the first "post-Christian" era in the United States. A Gallup poll from

March 2021 bears this out: only 47 percent of Americans said they belong to a church, down from 70 percent just twenty years ago.[2]

This decline is not only among young adults, of course, although postmortem considerations about the church's population loss often focus on those identified as millennials and members of Generation Z. Theories abound about why young people today show less connection to the church than at any other time in national history, even though some hypotheses seem based on little more than judgmental disregard for what the data suggests about younger generations and the church. According to these theories, young adults are too selfish, too self-centered, and too lazy to invest in a faith community. They are not joiners. They prefer to sleep in on Sundays or attend brunch with their friends. They've bought into the leftist lie that organized religion will forsake them. One claim making its rounds on the internet this past year asserted that young adults didn't go to church anymore because they were deeply mired in sexual sin, and attending church would only convict them to turn toward God, something they didn't want to do. In May 2021, a pastor tweeted to his ten thousand followers that people think of leaving the church mostly because they want to sleep with someone outside the confines of marriage. And an article in the *Gospel Coalition* suggests that young adults are "fornicating" more than ever and don't want the church to pry into their sex lives.[3]

Author Chrissy Stroop, writing for the website Flux, says that "the canard that the 'real' reason people leave Christianity is to embrace a 'life of sin' is an old standby in the apologist's bag of tricks."[4] Yet that standby has real traction, and some in my former church used it to justify the church's dissolution.

The argument went that those advocating for full inclusion of LGBTQIA people were merely hoping that the church might condone sins. People didn't want accountability, some said, and when church members asked that people be held accountable and avoid carnality, they simply fled rather than keep their baser nature in check. Those advocating for this viewpoint rarely, if ever, interrogate their own position, assuming instead that the Bible is absolutely clear in supporting their claims.

What struck me most in my church's dissolution was inflexibility on these points: that the Bible was clear about the sin of homosexuality; that LGBTQIA people could not be included in our community, unless they confessed their sin; that this issue was inviolate, and people had to choose to accept one theological position or be expelled from the church. Other disagreements in the church did not have the same purchase. Good people disagreed on several other theological positions: whether women could be in church leadership, whether Christians should be nationalistic, or whether the Bible advocated for some forms of nonresistance. No matter that these theological quandaries about gender equity and pacifism and one's allegiance to God had roots deep in the Quaker tradition. Such issues did not divide the church like the discussion on whether LGBTQIA folks might be fully included in the community. It is almost like it wasn't about the Bible's clarity after all.

Religion News Service reported in summer 2021 that young adults in other churches are experiencing what happened at my former Quaker church. A study by the Public Religion Research Institute reflected the exodus of young evangelicals from their churches because of "attitudes toward sexual minorities [that] are starkly at odds with their elders."[5] Far more young, white evangelicals support same-sex marriage, the article reported, than do their over-fifty white evangelical peers. For white evangelicals especially, but for other Christian groups as well, the predominant focus on Scripture's teaching on homosexuality to the exclusion of other verses on marriage and divorce, or the acquisition of wealth, or nationalism, means alienating young people who might wonder at the hypocrisy, and then decide to walk away.

In recent years, beliefs about the hypocrisy of organized religion have intensified, and not only regarding the inclusion of LGBTQIA people. As young adults become increasingly invested in issues of social justice, they see church leaders disengaged from fighting for racial and gender equity—and in some cases, not disengaged but outright hostile to movements intended to promote equity. After the murder of George Floyd, for example, thousands of young people took to the streets to protest his death and the killings of countless other Black people by police. Initially, it seemed that white evangelical leaders would denounce Floyd's murder, and a few major news outlets suggested that this might be an inflection point for Christians, with *The Atlantic* reporting in June 2020 that "the evangelical world is shifting [on race] in ways that would have been unimaginable only a few years ago."[6]

Such optimism faded when, in the same month, then president Donald Trump cleared Black Lives Matter protesters from Lafayette Square in Washington, DC, in order to awkwardly hold a Bible for a photo op in front of Saint John's Church. In the years since, white evangelicals have lined up to praise a man whom they see as the "most Christian president" in our national history, despite Trump's consistent use of racist tropes to appeal to his followers.[7] Some white evangelicals have denounced Black Lives Matter protesters, and insist that critical race theory—an interdisciplinary examination of how systemic racism was and is part of America's legacy—is being taught in schools, although it is rarely a part of K–12 curricula. Rather than seeking spaces for racial reconciliation, many white churches have insisted that racism no longer exists and that because God made only one race, the human race, fixation on racism is anti-biblical.

By early 2022, some Christian organizations, like the evangelical mouthpiece Focus on the Family, were publishing books and curricula teaching followers about the evils of critical race theory and how anti-racism efforts are ungodly, unchristian, and opposed to their biblical worldview, one that acknowledges racism as a personal sin, not a systemic one—a sin that can be remedied with confession. In this vein, the enslavement of people is seen only as a "flaw in the fabric of early American life," Focus on the Family writes. Because abolitionists who sought an end to slavery were Christian, America remains an exceptional nation, built by the goodness of Christian leaders who imagined a shining city on the hill.[8]

Many of the young people I interact with recognize the inadequacy of this rationale, and can articulate the challenges of an American exceptionalism ideal as well as acknowledge the presence of systemic racism that undermines any insistence on equity. They come by this worldview honestly, and not because their public schools indoctrinated them with critical race theory—something that was, until the past few years, a relatively obscure theory, as it is taught primarily in graduate and law schools. Growing up in the digital age has put most young adults in touch with a wide range of people, from a wide range of backgrounds. They've created diverse online communities. They see for themselves on TikTok and other streaming platforms that racism persists, not only on a personal but also a systemic level. They're using those same platforms to organize and protest injustice, with hashtags like #BlackLivesMatter connecting viewers to justice-minded content. It's easier to identify racism, including within one's community, when video after video shows alarming incidences of police officer violence or of white folks calling 911 when encountering Black people living their lives; or when, as happened in my small hometown in 2021, screenshots of teens "selling" their Black peers in an online "slave trade" are discovered and shared with nationwide audiences.[9]

Faced with this kind of digital evidence of racism, as well as their own lived experience, young adults who turn to the church for guidance on how to combat racism, hoping for a moral compass, have been disappointed by what they find, at least in white evangelicalism. While Black churches have consistently stepped into the fight for racial justice, too many white religious institutions have remained entrenched in white supremacy, believing that racism no longer exists; that their personal confession of sin means they are not accountable for racist acts; and that America was built not on slavery, but by an exceptionalism that reflects God's providence for a chosen people. When the church's definition of God's chosen people discounts the humanity of everyone save for those who are white, cisgender, and heterosexual, it's easy to see why so many young adults reject organized religion.

Churches might be inclined to believe that young people will be drawn back to the pews by flashy music and hip, tattooed pastors, or with a social media ministry that connects with the TikTok crowd, a repackaging of Jesus that resonates with a generation accustomed to rebranding now and then. But Brea Perry, writing for *The Witness: A Black Christian Collective*, has this to say about her generation's decision to stop attending church: she and her peers are not rejecting Jesus when they reject the church; instead, she writes, "we're leaving misogyny masquerading as mission, capitalism claiming to be calling, and narcissism naming itself fresh revelation."[10]

I'm awed by Perry's clarity and honesty. She willingly calls out church communities who have completely misestimated her generation, and rightly situates Jesus at the heart of faith, rather than the idols of patriarchy, nationalism, and capitalism. Though some in church communities will continue to wring their hands about kids these days abandoning church for a prodigal life, Perry challenges readers to consider whether they really know the Jesus they claim to serve. She provides an important reminder to those of us in relationship with young adults. We have a good deal to learn from their witness. Including, perhaps, that the faith of our fathers and our mothers will not suffice.

Another force driving an exodus from churches is the pursuit of justice in response to religious trauma. This term has gained prominence in the past decade because of social media and a growing awareness that some churches have caused immeasurable harm. Their theological positions and their willingness to exert emotional control over people on the margins inflicts further trauma on people who have been victimized. Movements like Church Too blossomed on social media platforms in 2017 after movie mogul Harvey Weinstein was accused of serial sexual assaults. Like the Me Too movement, which encouraged people, especially women, to share their stories of sexual abuse, those using the #ChurchToo hashtag described incidences of sexual assault and nonconsensual sexual advances in Christian environments.

Thousands of women (and some men) told their stories on social media of being harmed within a Christian context—in youth group, at summer camp, in church sanctuaries and Sunday school rooms—often expressing their outrage and grief that the very place where they should have felt safe traumatized them instead. Emily Joy Allison's 2021 book, *#ChurchToo*, takes Christian organizations to task for their untold sexual abuses, arguing that white evangelicals' obsession with purity culture has perpetuated more trauma. According to Allison, when the ideology of purity culture seeps deep into Christians' minds and bodies, they become perfect victims for assault. Purity culture is its own kind of grooming, and can be a precursor to assault. Young women in particular learn that their bodies are dangerous, and that they are the protector of men's presumable and sinful propensity to "stumble" when they encounter women. Concurrently, people hear time and again that sex is holy only within a marriage between a cisgender, heterosexual, monogamous husband and wife. Any other kind of sex is a paramount transgression against God that will potentially lead to a sinner's destruction.[11]

Given this overwhelming messaging, which likewise conveys that victimized people are complicit in perpetuating this grave sin, assault becomes a source of shame to be hidden. Thus, young people are less likely to report their assault to Christian leaders, and when they do, leaders are less likely to discipline abusers; leaders are also more likely to provide cover for abusers in their midst under the aegis of grace and forgiveness. Just one example that Allison provides is the *Houston Chronicle*'s 2019 exposé of the Southern Baptist Convention, which shielded church leaders who abused several hundred victims.[12] The SBC released a report in May 2022 showing how deep this abuse ran, and how leaders in the convention frequently protected abusers, shuttling them to new congregations when their abuse came to light or placing the onus of the abuse on victims, who were often silenced when they attempted to speak up.[13] The SBC's abysmal handling of the sexual assault cases reflects a fundamental pattern in church and parachurch organizations to stand with the accused rather than the accuser, further traumatizing those who have been abused.

For Alli, a twenty-three-year-old advocate for those experiencing homelessness, religious trauma was inflicted in part because of her youth group's hyper-focus on purity culture, which made her feel damaged and unworthy of love. She also felt alienated from the church because of its poor handling of her mental illness diagnosis. During her teen years, Alli attended a megachurch near her home, which she found "big and impersonal and cliquey." At thirteen, she started suffering from intense obsessive compulsive disorder, anxiety, and suicidal ideation.

Alli heard countless times from her church that if she only prayed, she could overcome the illness dominating her life. "I heard that anxiety was a sin because I wasn't trusting God enough," Alli said. "The only thing the church offered me was platitudes." One Sunday, a pastor told a story about a man possessed by "the demon of suicide," and how he was healed with prayer. The last straw was the pastor's joke, from the pulpit, that neurodivergent people in the church were like the body's appendix: part of the church body, sure, but no one knows what they do or why they're needed. Now, as a young adult, she doesn't call any church home. "Religious trauma is real," Alli said, "even though I still have a good relationship with Christ."

She voiced a common theme among young Christian adults. They believe in Jesus and consider themselves spiritual, but have been harmed by religious institutions which demand that Jesus followers must look, act, and think a specific way—one that many young people see as incompatible with their own worldview or biblical understanding. According to Jazmine, twenty-three, having a sincere relationship with Jesus remains important to her, and she feels that she is on good terms with Jesus. Still, attending church is difficult; she is gay, and she believes that "the entire political atmosphere" at so many churches will make it impossible for her to experience belonging in any congregation. Jazmine described having numerous conversations with people who, even if they continue to embrace the teachings of Jesus, are "choosing to walk away from the label Christian" because of the trauma Christians have caused in their lives.

This trauma is intrinsically tied to justice. Churches that alienate vulnerable people in their congregations and leadership that refuses to hold perpetrators accountable for the pain they've caused only reify unjust systems of power and control. Such churches also expose their craven hypocrisy, causing further disillusion for those seeking loving, Jesus-centered communities. One couple described how their sons' tenuous connection to the church was unraveled by a pastor they trusted, a pastor whose lack of sexual boundaries with the youth he served—and the lack of a robust response from church leaders—made their sons second-guess everything else the church said and did. Now they have no interest in attending church at all. These young adults are answering the call to justice, even when doing so means turning away from their family's deep commitments to organized faith. To them, and to others in their generation, the call to justice is that profound, that pressing, and is not being modeled in the churches that have traumatized them.

In Micah 6:3–5, the prophet imagines God in conflict with the people of Israel. Historically, Micah was addressing the people of the southern kingdom of Judah, who manifested a piety that outwardly suggested they were righteous followers of God. Yet Micah acknowledges that this seeming orthodoxy disguises the truth: the Judean people are far from God, and their righteousness is only a cover. The opening verses of Micah 6 voice God's reminder to the people of what has been done for them, how God delivered them from enslavement, guided them out of Egypt, provided liberation. God also sent worthy leaders, Aaron, Moses, and Miriam, the courageous prophet who, along with her brothers, freed the Israelites from their oppression. Shouldn't God's people remember all that God has done, leading them to a promised land, giving them well-being and a future?

In response, the Judeans ask how they are to repay God for their liberation. "With what shall I come before the Lord and bow down before the exalted God?" the speaker asks (Micah 6:6). Whether this question is asked in sincerity or irony is not wholly clear, though biblical scholars agree that the people's response lacks any real understanding of what reconciliation with God might look like. The interlocutor turns to the laws and commands of Scripture to suggest ways the people might be reconciled to God, and we must wonder at the profligacy, each line suggesting a greater offering, a deeper sacrifice: a thousand rams, ten thousand rivers of oil, even a firstborn son.

Despite the enormity of these suggestions—the willingness to relinquish a beloved son, the greatest sacrifice possible—God responds with incredulity. These offerings only reify the Judeans' orthodoxy, their sense that by following the laws and commands established by God, they will be reconciled to their Creator. Yet, Micah writes, God has already told the people what is required of them, not in the legalism of burnt offerings which amount to nothing, but through other means entirely: doing justice, loving mercy, walking humbly with God.

There's nothing new under the sun, truly.

Young people's decisions to leave church communities, but not their beliefs, reverberate in Micah's response. I see young adults' prophetic voices in my former church's conflict; I see them in the convulsive disruption occurring in other communities of faith, where people are insisting there can be only one path to righteous—the path they themselves have constructed, often on the backs of others. That way is formed through legalistic application of Scripture. Or, at least, of the scriptural passages they deem most significant. That way is formed around an insistence that Levitical commands should guide behavior.

That way says that what God requires from us is sacrifice, burnt offerings of rams, rivers of oil, the accoutrements of piety laid down on an altar. And not only that, but the sacrifice of identities integral to who young adults are, as queer or mentally ill or female or Black or Indigenous or any other identity that is not cisgender, not white, not male. Give that up, young people are told, relinquish who you are, for this is what God requires, a sacrifice that blunts your uniqueness. And if you can't meet that requirement, you need to confess your sin and change your identity. Only then will you be worthy of inclusion.

But God has already told us what is required, Micah responds, actions that manifest in love and justice and mercy, not in rigid rules that reflect only a patina of piety.

Finding our way forward with young adults requires embracing this call to justice outlined in Micah and echoed in the Gospels, where Jesus frequently notes that he stands with the dispossessed, the downtrodden, those on society's margins. In this, our young adults can lead us, and we can also be transformed, no longer simply embracing expressions of faith that do not serve all people well. We may need to concede that the traditional ways of doing church are not inviolate, and that those ways no longer work for many people who ardently believe in Jesus' words and his call for justice. Churches who refuse to refashion themselves—who insist that they will not capitulate to "social justice warriors" (as if being an advocate for social justice were a bad thing)—will, I imagine, sink into irrelevancy, their dying gasps muttering the so-called clobber verses they've used to build their impenetrable silos.

The young adults who have left the churches of their childhoods are rebuilding faith, with justice as a framework to guide their efforts. I see this play out on social media platforms, where young adults are crafting virtual communities that might well rival what some experience in churches. On Twitter, young adults are deconstructing the white evangelicalism of their childhoods, supporting each other as they tease out the gospel imperative of love and inclusion from the damaging messages of evangelical culture—messages premised on biblical interpretations that are likewise being deconstructed. Christian TikTok has coalesced around pastors and communities that challenge young adults to live out their faith apart from the strident political dogmas that color so much of evangelicalism today.

And some young adults are constructing their own kinds of worship experiences: Hiking together in nature they are working hard to protect because they profoundly feel God's presence there. Creating rituals in their homes to connect them to diverse communities that reflect the multifaceted image of God. Pursuing religious traditions more aligned with justice, or conflating several religious traditions into one, finding in the amalgam a new approach to knowing God. Several young adults told me that these unique pathways to a relationship with God have helped heal the trauma wrought by their evangelical upbringings, and that this healing might, at some point, take them back to church—though not the churches of their childhoods, the places that inflicted the trauma from which they are still trying to recover.

My own kids were just starting high school when their youth group scattered, torn apart by the church's divisions. The religious institutions of their childhood were no longer the same, including a beloved church camp, whose leadership decided against hiring those who believed in full inclusion for LGBTQIA people; this meant that some staff my kids adored were gone, exiled from the camp they'd served faithfully, in some cases for decades. After a lifetime spent in one congregation, the transition to a new church was difficult for Ben and Sam, as it was for other young people whose church home was gone. I know because I taught some of them in the subsequent years, and every one of them wrote about the church split as a defining moment in their lives, as a time when they saw faith, God, even their families differently.

Samuel took the division especially hard and lost any interest in church, no matter what it looked like. When COVID hit around their eighteenth birthdays, both boys stopped going to church; the pandemic forced us onto Zoom, and it was easier to let them sleep in on Sunday mornings than drag them to our living room and a small computer screen. They attended a smattering of outdoor socially distanced youth events that summer, but the pandemic completely severed their already tenuous connection to our new faith community, the one we'd turned to after the church split.

Some signs point to my sons' longing to know Jesus, even if they no longer attend church. Sam sends me TikTok videos of a pastor he follows on that platform, and I see in those clips my child's desire to not only connect with me on a spiritual plane, but also find sustenance in a charismatic Black preacher whose vibe speaks to Sam in a way Quaker worship never could. When he's home, I catch my other son singing praise choruses with his guitar or listening to Christian music on the car radio, and while that's not really how I find Jesus, I know that Benjamin's musicality and the connection to the church camp where he found his faith are represented in those songs and in the singing.

Whether either child makes his way back to organized religion remains to be seen. I hope that they, like others in their generation, will find a deeper faith, one focused on Jesus and his teachings, on the Creator's encompassing love rather than on God's judgment, on the work to which we are all called: to do justice, love mercy, and walk with humility. After all, discovering a deeper faith with the young adults we love means having faith that God holds them still, even when they reject churches that have done little to make them feel welcomed and known.

Despite the heartache of our church split and the pain it caused my own beloved children, I'm grateful for the young people I watched in the balcony several years ago, and for their model of faithful justice at work even when they were being traumatized by those who would deny their humanity. I am confident that they will rise up to create a far more just world, one that reflects the glory and beautiful diversity of God's kingdom. It's up to us, their teachers and mentors and parents, to follow their lead.

SHORT EXERCISES

1. Think about your relationship to the church when you were a young adult. How did you feel nurtured by your church experience? How did you feel alienated? How might your experience create openings for conversations about faith with the young adults you love?

2. Explore social media platforms where young Christians are finding communities. What about these platforms might appeal to young adults? How could you use discussions about these platforms to build a bridge to the young adults in your life?

3. What are some practical ways you can encourage faith communities in your area to do justice? How can you invite young people to work with you in these initiatives?

EIGHT

To a More Perfect Kind of Love

The Tarzan swing in Monteverde is the kind of ubiquitous attraction in Costa Rica meant to enchant Western tourists. Apparently, the rainforest, volcanos, beaches, wild animals, and exotic birds are not enough to draw people to this part of Central America. Instead, tourists can learn about the country's unique ecosystem and rich culture by zip-lining, riding ATVs, and jumping off forty-five-meter-high platforms to swing like Tarzan through a jungle.

Two days before encountering the Tarzan swing, I had arrived in Costa Rica along with twenty-three other women from George Fox University: twenty-two students and one coleader, Jill, who was a close friend of several decades and who teaches math at the college. Each May since the late 1980s, the university has offered overseas travel to its junior students, a three-week international trip subsidized by the institution. I'd last led Juniors Abroad in 2001, shortly after beginning my career, and a year before the arrival of Benjamin. Once Ben was in my life, and then Sam, I'd turned down invitations to lead Juniors Abroad trips, knowing that twenty-one days away from my family was about eighteen days too many.

But my kids were all grown up now, out of the house and experiencing their own adventures. Because I'd resolved to say yes more often to new opportunities, I agreed to colead the trip, especially if Jill came along. It was a fluke that only women had signed up for the tour of Costa Rica that Jill and I agreed to lead, but we saw this as a happy circumstance. The dynamics of an all-women troupe offered intriguing possibility: more potential to be fully ourselves without the pressure to perform for any men in our midst. Just a group of women being adventurous and facing up to new experiences, including a different culture, unfamiliar food, physical challenges, and for me, a Tarzan swing.

Here's something you may have already figured out from reading this book. I am a fearful person, anxious about a good many things. For the most recent stretch of my existence, I've tried to control my uncontrollable thoughts with behavioral therapy, to some degree of success. Like most fearful people, I can hide my phobias well, until I encounter them directly, in which case I become a sweaty, shaky mess.

Back in the early years of my marriage, I almost let my anxieties win. As Ron and I contemplated creating a family, through birth or through adoption, my anxious mind reminded me of what raising children would entail—a nearly constant encounter with my fears. I would have to choose:

children or my phobias. Raising my boys has introduced me to fears I couldn't even fathom way back in the early aughts when we were making decisions about our family, but I'm profoundly grateful I didn't concede to fear.

As I considered a trip to Costa Rica and Panama, I faced all those questions again about whether I wanted to confront my fears. I knew there would be volcano hikes, canopy walks on bridges above rainforests, and zip-lining, and being afraid of heights is one of many fears I hold close to my heart. Except when I'm up too high, whereupon my heart thrums loudly, announcing to anyone who notices that I'm preparing to die. I also worried that a trip with twenty-two students who were eating unfamiliar food and potentially succumbing to the motion sickness of boat rides and mountain roads might mean needing to care for barfing young women. As an emetophobe, someone who fears vomit, this seemed a potentially disastrous outcome.[1]

Still, I said yes to the trip, and to facing these fears. Which is why, two days into our journey, I stood before an abyss, strapped into a Tarzan swing, deciding whether I could jump.

There is so much to fear right now, so many weighty stressors, that my own phobias seem paltry by comparison. When I talk about my phobias with others (a rare occurrence, if I'm honest), I'm embarrassed by how negligible these fears seem, given the grave forces some people face. In *Fight: How Gen Z Is Channeling Their Fear and Passion to Save America*, data journalist John Della Volpe begins this way:

These are the words and phrases Generation Z use to paint the picture of the America that raised them:

terrifying

broken

declining

fake

close-minded

divided

aggressive

dystopia

off the rails

a bloody mess.[2]

Volpe's work on the Harvard Public Opinion Project has connected him to the pulse of Gen Z through polling and focus groups, and that pulse is racing because of the many stressors young adults now encounter. He notes that nearly half of all young adults are now receiving treatment for depressive symptoms, that suicide rates have skyrocketed in recent years, and that this generation's mental health issues are overwhelming an already burdened healthcare system.[3]

Some people grouse about kids these days being too coddled. But this mythology about weak-willed young adults is not supported by the data, despite the prevailing narrative that helicopter parents have protected their children from every potential challenge, making young people into snowflakes who melt under pressure. An oft-quoted book by Jeremy Adams about Gen Z, published in 2021, says that young adults today are "hollowed-out zombies" "barren of the behavior, values and hopes from which human beings have traditionally found higher meaning . . . or even simple contentment."[4] Other writers echo Adams's critique, blaming technology, the dissolution of nuclear families, and the weakening of religious communities for the burgeoning mental health crises among young adults.

Such uncharitable claims fail to recognize that there are good reasons for the stress experienced by members of Gen Z—nor do these critiques acknowledge the role that older generations play in contributing to the struggles young adults face. We've already explored some stressors: the pressures they feel to be successful, to make their one "wild and precious life" productive; the fraying of their faith communities and the hypocrisy they see predominating in churches who profess Jesus as savior; the isolation they experience, accelerated by the siloing influence of social media and other technologies.

They are also challenged by the persistent threat to their very lives.

Even before COVID-19 wiped out several years of a normal young adulthood and killed millions of people worldwide, gun culture in the United States had caused a preponderance of mass shootings that make any seemingly safe space a potential crime scene. In a 2018 Harris poll, initiated by the American Psychological Association, nearly 75 percent of Gen Z respondents saw mass shootings as a persistent threat. In the years since that poll, the prevalence of gun violence has only increased.[5] The *Washington Post* reports that in the first six months of 2022, there wasn't a week without a mass shooting in the United States; in 2021, there were nearly seven hundred incidences when four or more people were gunned down.[6] Young people spent their childhoods checking the exits to any place they entered, a tactic they learned during active shooter drills in schools. A reminder of the threat they face is present even in the way schools are now constructed.

At my institution, our classroom doors have special locks to block an armed intruder, and it is almost impossible to get into classrooms using doors that open to the quad—a reality we didn't have to deal with even ten years ago. We face our mortality each time we step into a classroom and see those locks, and even attending a writing class can be a fear-filled proposition.

Political extremism is also on the rise. The parents and grandparents of today's young adults vaguely feared violence from foreign actors—like other Gen Xers, I knew that Russia might attack the United States, the duck-and-cover drills we practiced a supposed safeguard against the kind of nuclear apocalypse portrayed in the 1983 television film *The Day After*. While wars and rumors of war persist, the threat of violence feels even closer now. Recent bulletins from the Department of Homeland Security warn of domestic terrorist attacks and the need to remain vigilant while in "soft target" areas, including schools, music and sporting event venues, and places of worship. Extremist groups like Patriot Front and the Proud Boys are especially pernicious in promoting violence to progress their racist ideologies, stoking fear especially in Black and brown communities and among LGBTQIA people.

Social media networks provide easy back channels for communication among political extremists, allowing for coordination and connection. According to Volpe, "media environments knowingly offer [extremist groups] oxygen in exchange for ad revenue, cable ratings, and chits in a cultural war."[7] Far-right and -left organizations have also preyed on Gen Z, using their vulnerabilities, like loneliness and mistrust of authority, to increase membership, especially among white cisgender young men who believe they have been marginalized by an increasingly diverse society. In an interview with *Mother Jones*, sociologist Michael Kimmel noted that extremist groups attract "guys [who] believe something has been taken from them that they were entitled to, that they deserved, and it was given to people who don't deserve it, like immigrants and gay people and women."[8] Fear of irrelevance, of being "replaced," has stoked young men's anger, reflected in recent mass shootings where marginalized groups were specifically targeted by young, often white, men.

Members of the Proud Boys came to my small hometown in 2021, staging a counterprotest to one organized by local advocates seeking to support students in our school district. Earlier that year, the school board had written policies demanding that teachers remove any "political or quasi-political" flags from their classrooms, including Black Lives Matter or LGBTQIA signs. The peaceful protest against the policy at Newberg's center flared into heated exchanges when the Proud Boys filtered in, trying to claim space already held by community members. I watched as a student wrapped in a gay pride flag stood her ground against a man who first menaced her, then shoved her to the ground. The air was charged, and I worried that someone carrying a weapon might explode. No deadly violence occurred, but the event was traumatizing, even for someone like me, a cisgender white woman with significant privilege.

In class the following day, I mentioned the rally, how unsettling it all seemed, how impressed I was with George Fox students for standing up against bigotry and hate. Two days later, a Black student approached me, admitting she hadn't known the Proud Boys were in town, and my mention of their presence near our campus had caused her anxiety to spiral. She'd chosen our university because the town felt safe, and now, Proud Boys were almost at her doorstep, threatening to do harm. She wondered why no one at the university had told her about the rally and expressed frustration that she'd only heard about the protest in the middle of first-year composition. At a majority-white campus, and in a majority-white town, the student was on high alert, worried that her life was imperiled because she was Black. I was reminded again that my young queer, Black, and brown students face threats to their safety in ways that I and many others in my small town rarely do.

Especially for those on the margins, any space—even what seems like a placid campus, nestled in a quiet small town—can be menacing.

These violent threats affect us all, of course.

My boys were at church camp when an active shooter entered a movie theater in Aurora, Colorado, in 2012, killing twelve and injuring another seventy people who were watching *The Dark Knight Rises*. When I heard the news, I wanted to drive immediately to the coastal camp and retrieve my kids. If such horrific carnage could visit a random movie theater, who was to say whether another deranged shooter might step off Highway 101 and into the camp mess hall, where my sons might be an easy target.

Later that same year, I went to the school pickup line hours after the Sandy Hook shooting. A twenty-year-old gunman had killed twenty-six people, including twenty first-graders, in Connecticut, thousands of miles away, but way too close to home. My kids were in fifth grade that year, and I remember crying when they came busting out the school door, oblivious to what had happened. That night, dropping them off at a friend's birthday party, I stood with other mothers on a front porch, weeping about what was lost, the pain other families were experiencing just then. After each shooting—an all too regular occurrence now—my first thoughts turn to parents whose children are senselessly gone, a devastation I cannot even imagine but now fear might become my reality too.

That my sons both have brown skin adds another layer of fear for me as a parent. In 2021, a Pew survey noted that 81 percent of Asian Americans reported an increase in violence against them, scapegoated because COVID-19 presumably originated in China; when I hear news about racially motivated attacks targeting Asian Americans, I think first of Benjamin, and then of his fiancé Kelcie, and their vulnerability as young people who are Asian.[9] Samuel, who was born in India, identifies as Black, and every time I hear about another Black man killed by police, my heart turns to my son. I am terrified that his sometimes insouciant demeanor toward authority could turn a traffic stop deadly. In a country where police brutality threatens the lives and security of Black and brown people, especially Black men, I worry that my son doesn't think enough about the snap judgments that police might make about his appearance.

As my sons grew older and developed more independence, I felt that the threats to their well-being multiplied, as did my fear. I was tempted to lecture them each time they left the house about the choices they made, how they drove their cars, whether they should spend time with friends I distrusted, whether they were being vigilant in public about the possibility of active shooters. Even now, with my sons living several thousand miles away, it's easy to want to microman-age their lives, to seek their assurance that they are keeping themselves safe. I'm sure other parents feel similarly, whether their kids are miles from home or living under the same roof. Because when every place seems threatening, we might want to demand they remain guarded by their parents and the illu-sory sense of security we think we can provide.

In these moments, we all face a choice: give in to our fears and keep our kids cloistered, always in our purview and thus our control, or let go, trusting they will do their best to remain safe and praying for God's protection over them in what often seems a malevolent world. But we face not only that choice, but another one as well. We can be paralyzed by fear, certain that nothing we do can make a difference. Or, following the lead of today's young adults, we can fight with all we've got to make that malevolence obsolete, using love to drive out fear.

Less than a year after my sons' graduation, both kids were living under my roof again after some time spent away, and several friends had joined them, using our sons' rooms as home base. That summer, Oregon recorded its highest temperatures ever, and for a while, the heat turned deadly, 110 degrees Fahrenheit one day, a few clicks hotter the next. Oregonians aren't built for this kind of weather, nor are their houses, and everyone slumped through each day, edgy and irritable. My anxiety as a parent seemed especially pointed that month, with one son declaring his intent to become an Army infantryman, the tip of the spear for armed combat, and the other insisting he be treated as an adult, but with-out assuming responsibilities attached to that role. One of the young men living with us said that he and my son "just wanted to live their lives," though his manifesto of liberation meant living their lives on our dime—a dime earned, in part, through the extra work I'd taken on that summer.

I was hot, and miserable, and so, so sad. Also, lost: I didn't know what I could do, what my family could do, to help my children find their way to independence, nor to change the conditions of the world we'd created. Whatever I was doing currently wasn't the right approach, and my attempt to micromanage my now adult sons only added to the sense of perpetual conflict in our family. Welcoming more young men to stay with us was only making things worse; they had nowhere else to go, my sons claimed, and some nights, we had five extra bodies staying in our bonus room. My husband and I often felt like visitors to our own home, overtaken by teenagers who cruised through our kitchen looking for food but offered us little in return for our hospitality.

One afternoon, when the heat spell had finally broken and we could breathe, I decided to clear some brush in our back yard by myself, even though capable young men were at that moment inside the house, no doubt playing video games. Their willingness to let me do all the yard work in addition to my salaried job fueled my building ire, and I decided that using a chainsaw might blunt my pointed anger. I revved up the machine and went to work on some rhododendrons that had been mauled by a redwood plummeting into our yard the previous fall. The woodcutting therapy started to work, and I felt satisfaction, relief, as the chainsaw blade cut through each dead branch.

Until a bird started dive-bombing me, squawking, insistent that I leave. When I finally relented and stepped away from the brush, I saw under my foot the ruins of a nest, and three baby birds I'd crushed beneath my feet. One was still gasping for breath; the other two were clearly dead already. Even now, a year later, I cannot think about that moment without a cavern of grief opening inside me for what I did to those babies and especially for what I did to the mother, desperate to save her tiny offspring. That day I found my husband, working elsewhere in the yard, and started sobbing, gulping out, "I didn't mean to kill them. I didn't see them. I'm so sorry." Was I apologizing to the mother bird? To my husband? To the universe? I didn't know, but wept episodically the rest of that day, unbelieving that I'd taken the life of three birds on the cusp of leaving their nest.

For both Ron and me, good Quakers that we are, this incident brought to mind the abolitionist John Woolman. In his *Journal*, Woolman writes about a pivotal moment in his life when, as a child, he threw rocks at a robin's nest, killing the mother robin. He was immediately remorseful, realizing that the hatchlings in the nest would not survive without their mother, so he retrieved the nest and killed the babies as well. Consumed by guilt, and in acknowledgment of this "wicked" deed, Woolman decided from that point forward that he should "exercise goodness towards every living creature."[10]

Woolman's epiphany informed his ministry and witness, as well as his abolition work. And while I don't believe I needed my hulking feet to step on a wren's nest to learn my lesson, killing the baby birds and my outsize response to their death compelled me to think with more clarity about the mountain of fear consuming me: for my kids' seeming aimlessness, for the chaotic and broken world, for my inability to help others find their way. That night, at a once-a-month parenting group I attended, I confessed my sadness, wondering at the symbolism of baby birds squashed beneath my feet. Was I stepping on my kids too? Were my fears and my anxiety about their futures keeping them from being who God created them to be? How did I also need to "exercise goodness towards every living creature"?

Despite my fear-driven desire to monitor my kids and to remain in control, I couldn't guarantee their security. For the past year, I'd been far too invested in their decision-making, nearly every waking moment spent perseverating about where my boys were, what they were doing, whether they were making wise decisions for what I saw as their flourishing. The heft of this emotional labor left me exhausted and brittle, my thoughts consumed by fear for them. I saw threats everywhere. In the racial unrest that might encircle them. In the climate crisis they would inherit. In the toxic social media environment enrapturing them. And in my elder son's interest in guns and war, as well as his willingness to support institutions that were contributing to bloodshed.

If any of us were to survive, metaphorically at least, I needed to change my heart and mind. Moment by moment, I prayed earnestly for the will and wisdom to transform my mindset and my immobilizing fear. My prayers became a plaintive refrain of *Please God please God please God*, though I recognized that I needed to also pray, *Not my will, but yours be done.*

There is no fear in love, but perfect love drives out fear. That summer, I tried hard to understand what this passage from 1 John 4:18 means, reading it over and over again. I googled the verse, seeking interpretations, and came up with sometimes trite, sometimes contradictory answers. Searching for "fear" and "love" called up several memes, but nothing to help me see. So I turned to the people I trust, the pastors and thinkers who have helped my faith most. What they told me boiled down to this: God loves us perfectly, and calls us to love others too. When we live in fear—fear of others, fear of the future, fear of ourselves—we are unable to love with the wholeheartedness to which we are called. This fulsome love was demonstrated in the ministry of Jesus in the Gospels, who despite expressing fear (*My God, my God, why have you forsaken me?*), chose radical love for all God's children.

Perfect love casts out fear. To love others well, I needed to let go of my fear. This was my own Woolmanesque epiphany, one that found my praying arms open to God, a physical manifestation of what I needed to do: release my sons from my fear, allowing them to live a life apart from mine, to chart their own futures, to rise and fall on their own choices. Letting go of that sense of security was one of the hardest things I've done as a parent. But in the moment, it also seemed like one of the most loving. If I relinquished my sense of control and they left our home, I would miss them intensely, and my own identity might need to shift in their absence. The way forward seemed clear, though, and in another series of grueling conversations, I told each of them that I thought leaving Newberg might be the best way for them to find themselves, to grow up, to become men.

Less than one month later, Samuel moved away to work in the hospitality industry. Two months later, Benjamin enlisted. My heart aches in their absence, and at times I have felt unmoored, the house a constant reminder of our changed circumstances. This might seem like a too perfect ending to this story, but it's true: as they started to thrive away from home, my fears for them and for their futures diminished.

Mostly.

I would guess anyone who closely engages with young people knows the contours of prayer intimately. Some days, prayer might seem like the only real act we can take to support the young adults we love, our earnest supplications for their safety and well-being a desperate attempt to grasp a semblance of control. We may not be able to guide their steps as we once did, so we turn to prayer, passing on to God the role of protector we sometimes assume is primarily ours.

My prayer life has never been richer than in the past few years, because my children were becoming adults and I have sometimes felt an acute need for divine intervention in their lives. Prayers also seem increasingly urgent because of the state of our world. So much of our environment appears well beyond our control, especially when safe spaces no longer feel safe, when a man can walk into a church sanctuary, or a movie theater, or a night club, or a grocery store and begin firing at will. In this chaos, this unknowing, we tend to ameliorate our fear by trying to exert control, making our environment knowable again.

And praying, with desperation, that things might change, that we could return to *the way things were*, when we could go into a grocery store unconcerned about a deadly virus or the specter of an active shooter. (Though, of course for some, *the way things were* was never safe or predictable in the first place.) Anne Lamott, writing about prayer for the *New York Times*, noted that many of us are "absolutely undone" by the world's tragedies. Her only recourse in the face of so much human misery is to "listen, commiserate, and offer to pray." We cannot alleviate everyone's pain, fear, and suffering, Lamott says, but "by opening my heart to someone in trouble, I create with them more love, less of a grippy clench in our little corner of the universe."[11] For Lamott, for me, and for countless others, prayer is one antidote to the chaos we confront every day. Our earnest hope is that the people we love most will feel heard and loved and protected through our prayers.

Still, younger people see with clearer eyes the ways our earnest prayers may not be enough. After every mass shooting, politicians send out their thoughts and prayers to victims of the tragedy, an impulse so ubiquitous that the gesture now seems pro forma because those thoughts and prayers are never followed by meaningful action that might make young people safer. In the aftermath of the school shooting in Uvalde, Texas, in May 2022, one young adult wrote the cry of her generation: "Gen Z is done with just 'thoughts and prayers.'" The writer Gabrielle Abdelmessiah notes the ways gun violence has shaped her generation, critiques the performative empathy of her elders, and argues that her peers will one day soon be "obtaining positions of power" and "will not tolerate" the chaos, the violence, the empty prayers, the lack of substantive change any longer.[12]

Bryce Colefield, an activist in Oregon, preached at my church about the need for people to "pray with their feet," echoing the words of Rabbi Abraham Joshua Heschel, who spoke these words after a voting rights march from Selma to Montgomery in 1965. Many young adults like Colefield see clearly that the old ways of living were not just, equitable, or loving. Because they've survived in a world beset by chaos, they tend to know that any sense of control is a chimera. Instead of giving way to fear, though, so many are charged with optimism, a belief that the world they are creating can be a better place, one where far more of us can flourish and become who God has created us to be. This generation gives me hope because they have so much to teach us. They are reforming society and culture through their creativity, activism, and compassion, and with the same foundational belief John Woolman expressed, that every living creature deserves to be treated with the utmost kindness.

Whether they are believers or not, members of Gen Z are praying with their feet. Despite facing innumerable threats to their lives, young adults are not necessarily paralyzed with fear, hunkering down in their homes to avoid the very real possibility of random mass shootings or race-based aggression. Instead, despite their anxieties, they are working hard to make change. For example, in the aftermath of the shooting at Marjory Stoneman Douglas High School in Parkland, Florida, in 2017, young people—especially those directly traumatized by that event—responded with courage and resolve. Within a month, several students from Marjory Stoneman Douglas had mobilized, organizing March for Our Lives, a demonstration for gun control that took place in Washington, DC, and at over eight hundred other sites worldwide.

Another event was planned five years later in the wake of the shooting at Robb Elementary in Uvalde, Texas, that left nineteen students and two teachers dead. A founder of March for Our Lives (and a victim of the Marjory Stoneman shooting) noted that young people are responsible for a lot of advocacy in the United States. "We have our whole lives ahead of us, and we don't want to live the rest of our days in fear," she said in an interview. Young people are often the ones who are targeted in school shootings. And they are "uniquely creative and equipped" to organize and build relationships with each other both virtually and in person.[13] Their efforts might be working; for the first time in three decades, a bipartisan gun control bill was passed in the US Capitol, potentially making the world safer for subsequent generations.

Some young adults are also redefining the terms of activism, using the digital tools they've grown up with to amplify causes and creatively confront those who abuse their power. Some notable examples: In 2020, young adults reserved thousands of free tickets for a Trump rally in Tulsa, Oklahoma, ghosting the then president at the actual event. For a president hyper-focused on his audience size, showing up to an emptier arena than he had planned was deeply embarrassing. Organizers have also relied on TikTok and other social media platforms to call out racism and misogyny, and to press for environmental policies that might slow the disastrous effects of climate change. An organization called Gen Z for Change has helped mobilize young adults, and in the past year, Gen Z for Change led an effort to flood a Virginia state tip line set up to report "woke" teachers who were discussing critical race theory, and overwhelmed Starbucks with eighty-eight thousand fake job applications after the company fired several employees who were trying to unionize.[14] In July 2022, a member of Gen Z for Change, Olivia Julianna, fundraised nearly $2 million for reproductive rights the day after a Florida congressman fat-shamed her on his Twitter feed, doubling down on his comment that pro-choice women are "odious" in their appearance.[15] Rather than succumbing to fear, these young people are choosing justice, a significant means of expressing love for their neighbors by relying on the tools they know intimately.

I've witnessed the ingenuity and energy of young adults in my community as they push institutions to become more inclusive; as they confront the racism and misogyny they've experienced in classrooms and church sanctuaries; as they call their elders to account for failing to consider their safety and well-being. Over the past few years, many of my journalism students have turned to their writing to promote justice and equity, reporting on the struggles LGBTQIA people face at Christian universities, the challenging stigma of having a mental illness diagnosis, the benign and overt misogyny they've experienced in male-dominated fields. Some of this work has subsequently been published, an amplification that reflects the maturity and passion of these student voices.

Given the state of the world, we may be tempted to despair, but I hope we will remember this. The passion and creativity of young adults can help save us, if only we relinquish control of what we think they should be doing and how they should be responding to the fears they face. If only we let go of our golden calves, those ways of being that we believe are inviolate. If only we allow them to teach us.

If only we pray with our feet too.

This is hard work, requiring a good bit of courage, trust in those far younger than us, and a willingness to relinquish paralyzing fear, revising our mindsets to recognize that there is more than one way to change the world. In other words, striving for the perfect love of God, the kind that drives out fear.

The trip to Costa Rica was made possible because the young adults I love most are no longer in my home, no longer needing me in the same ways. But being there with twenty-two college students reminded me again of the many reasons I love working with young adults. Jill and I had gotten to know our students, but just barely, in an every-other-week class during the spring semester. We flew to San José two days after graduation, and I spent the first few hours of the trip trying to figure out who these women were, if only in terms of their names and not much more.

For three weeks, we drove around Central America in a tourist bus, stayed in hotels too rustic for my liking, ate more beans and rice than I had since graduate school. We saw sloths. We escaped a scrum of hangry monkeys. We snorkeled in the Pacific Ocean and the Caribbean Sea. And we talked, long conversations on the bus and at dinner and into the night. I listened to the students' stories, how their fearful, wonderful lives bore witness to the grace of God. As the days passed, I started seeing the students' individual identities emerging, and this unwinding was an absolutely delight. It was easy to see how each woman might be deeply cherished by the adults in her life, and to admire the thoughtful, complex, funny, loving ways the women interacted with others. Their wide-eyed wonder at what they were seeing made me likewise open to wonder; their adventurous spirit loosened my own tight-fisted trepidation. I found myself trying new activities, new food, new conversations because they seemed so willing themselves to explore.

We were all out of our element, but they were teaching me what it means to live abundantly and with courage. This was a lesson that started in Monteverde with the Tarzan swing, which comes at the end of a zip line course that includes the longest line in Central America, almost a mile of cable stretched over a canyon. Some students took the final line Superman style, on their stomachs with arms outstretched, allowing them to look over the tree canopy as they zoomed by. I'd shown significant fortitude in each of the first nine lines and decided that trying Superman would be a bridge—or really, a line—too far. I settled for the traditional way of zipping, if there were such a thing, then somehow managed to strand myself a few hundred feet short of the platform, meaning I had to work my way to the end hand over hand like a monkey.

By the time I reached the Tarzan swing, other students and my coleader had already taken the plunge, and they stood arrayed at the bottom of the forty-five-meter platform, necks craned upward to watch me walk across a suspension bridge, then have my safety gear checked by the young men near the platform's edge. The women knew my fear of heights—I'd said something about that fear repeatedly during the previous semester—and began cheering for me, as if I were a hero for making the attempt. My body's every cell wanted me to give up, to head back toward safety. I sensed there wasn't any turning back, though.

Isn't that always true, that we cannot go backward? We can't return to the world we've known before, the one that seemed safer for some of us, less chaotic. Time moves on, and each day we are faced with new opportunities to make a different world, one built with kindness for every living creature in mind, the frame constructed with justice and equity and God's perfect love. Rather than longing for some past, we are invited to walk forward, following young adults and their passion, praying with our feet as we've never prayed before.

In Costa Rica, I knew my fear was dwarfed by bigger problems in the world, and my courage in the face of a Tarzan swing has nothing on the many challenges that young adults face now. Still, in the moment with twenty-two young adults cheering, the symbolism wasn't lost on me. This universe is so difficult, the forces against each of us sometimes overwhelming, but we are all part of this "beautiful and terrible" party that Frederick Buechner describes, so perfectly created and loved by God that the world cannot exist without each one of us in it. We can choose fear and retreat or take a leap forward into the abundant life this world offers us.

I stood at the edge of the platform, peering out over the humid jungle, sweat adhering my shirt to my back. "I really can't do this," I said. "No, no, no, I really can't." I looked down at the distance to the ground, the vast open space ahead of me. My students, too far away, couldn't register the abject fear paralyzing me. They continued to yell, an invocation assuring me that, like them, I could face down this challenge.

I've never believed those who confess that life flashed before their eyes in near-death experiences. I don't believe it now, even though the Tarzan swing stoked my intense fear of plummeting to my death from an incomprehensible height. Yet in that crucible moment when I had to decide whether I could face my fears and jump, I thought not about my life but about the rustic hotel I'd return to, triumphant or not. About the social media post I'd write if I succeeded in jumping, and the one I wouldn't post if I failed. About the bold young women cheering in the jungle below, how they'd already inspired me to face our trip with unflinching resolve.

The swing operators told me how I needed to hold my body, where I needed to put my hands. They showed me again that everything was secure, the safety equipment engaged properly. I heard the chorus below calling me out by name, their voices giddy from jumps already finished.

"I don't think I can do this," I said again.

"You need to change your mindset, then," one of the young workers said.

Hadn't I done that already, a million times and more, ever since Ben and Sam were babies, my life turned upside down in all the best ways? I thought about my beautiful boys, brilliant and reckless and brave and maddening, the brightest and best gifts I'd ever received. They'd throw themselves from the swing platform, I was sure of it, with the same fearlessness that had characterized their young adulthood, with the courage they'd manifested in leaving home for their unknown futures.

Like them, like all of us, I had a choice to make, one that would require a changed mindset. Could I do it? Even then, I didn't know.

"Pura vida!" the young worker exclaimed. *Pura vida*: the Costa Rican affirmation that all is well, that all will be well, that this life is worth living. He opened the platform gate, inviting me to leap.

SHORT EXERCISES

1. What are some of your biggest fears for the young adults in your life? Reflect on those fears and on ways you might use those fears as an impetus to help mitigate those threats.

2. Consider some ways you might pray with your feet, then make a specific plan that puts prayer into action. (And then, perhaps, follow through with this plan.)

3. What does perfect love look like for you? How have you understood the idea that "perfect love drives out fear"?

Epilogue

My oldest niece gave birth this year. Leah's pregnancy had not been easy, and when she entered the hospital for an induction, we all waited anxiously for news out of Indiana, cousins and grandparents and aunts and uncles checking in on our family's Facebook group chat for word of Hadley Suzannah's arrival.

The wait was a long one, and several days of labor stretched out until the pictures of a baby landed in the group chat alongside news that although Leah had a challenging delivery, she would be okay. I thought about my little sister, Amy, at the hospital with her child, and I wondered about how stressful it must have been to witness a daughter struggling through abundant hours of hard labor.

Amy is in another liminal space now, her youngest having graduated from college and her oldest starting a new family, making my sister a grandma. Time's current rushes on, and the next generation is assuming the roles we played only minutes ago, so it seems. I see that current manifest on social media, images of solidly middle-aged people who once inhabited my classrooms at George Fox. How did that even happen? My eldest son will be married soon, with imminent plans to start a family, a circle of life spinning at warp speed.

But at the moment, our extended family was focused on the arrival of Hadley Suzannah, my parents' first great-grandchild. As we celebrated Hadley, I wondered at the immense love poured into a baby girl, an expansive network of people across the continent, expressing unalloyed joy for someone even her parents don't fully know yet. That love was manifest in a Facebook group, in the anxious waiting for someone, a stranger really, to arrive. Her new parents, Leah and Sawyer, will spend their entire lifetimes, if they are lucky, learning about this new being they've brought into the world, the little person so ardently cherished before she was even here.

It's such a mysterious, awe-filled thing, this kind of love. Most parents experience it in one way or another from the moment they meet their children, if not before their child is placed in their arms. I felt that deep well of love for Benjamin Quan and Samuel Saurabh when we received their referral pictures, long before their adoptions. I looked into their brown eyes and knew indubitably that these were my sons, the people I'd been called to raise. We had turned away from other adoption referrals, for no other reason than that those children didn't seem like our son or daughter. I can't explain the initial rush of love for Benjamin and Samuel beyond that, and while I don't believe *God has a plan* and *everything happens for a reason*, I do know that when Benjamin's and

Samuel's pictures hit my email inbox, my love for them was already immense, more powerful than any love I'd ever experienced before.

This reflects our inherent worth, this deep love, this sense that someone comes into the world beloved, a gift from God that calls for our rejoicing. Not every child receives that enormity of love on earth, which is in itself a humbling thought. But we are all worthy of it, and our rejoicing with a newborn should continue throughout each person's life, their presence a reminder that their very creation is a blessing. The power of that love should bring us to our knees in gratitude, compelling us to ensure that every human is treated with the honor and glory we all deserve.

Imagine living with the kind of rejoicing we often reserve for newborns, and with the acknowledgment that we are all fearfully, wonderfully made, formed by the grace of God in a world uniquely created for each of us. Imagine if we could all fearlessly live the inconvertible truth of the Gospels, that we deserve grace, and hope, and justice, and peace. Imagine believing we are worth this deepest-felt rejoicing, whether we're adults trying to do our best or young people seeking traction into their futures or a little girl named Hadley Susannah who just recently made her entrance in the world. She will be a young adult soon enough, and then—as now— she deserves the deepest, most profound love of God we can offer her.

ACKNOWLEDGMENTS

I never really understood those who responded negatively to the idea that it takes a village to raise up a child, though I remember when a First Lady wrote a book with that title in the 1990s and people responded with outrage, insisting that a child needed only her parents to raise her right. Even before I became a mom, I knew kids needed a village to thrive, probably because the villages I'd experienced as a young person helped me flourish.

And now, in my twenty-some years of parenting, my village has played an integral role in who my sons have become. I am exceedingly grateful for the many people in this village who have loved Benjamin and Samuel well. I have confidence that my kids will find their way to settled adulthood because of others who expressed love for Jesus through their love for my kids, and for me: their Sunday school teachers, camp counselors, youth pastors, teachers and coaches, baseball and soccer moms, grandparents, aunts and uncles, siblings. Our village has been substantial, and I'm thankful for that largesse, well aware that not everyone has the same access to so much support.

It also takes a village to write a book, and I'm grateful for the many ways I've been encouraged through the process of completing this project. This support starts with my agent, Jevon Bolden of Emboldened Media Group, who gave me confidence when I had none, and has helped me become more of the writer God intended me to be. (Shout-out to Collegeville Institute for introducing me to Jevon and a dozen other stunningly talented women, whom I met at a summer workshop in 2019.) I'm also grateful for the Herald Press editorial team, including Laura Leonard, Elisabeth Ivey, Sara Versluis, and Amy Gingerich; working with you all is always a joy.

This project could not have happened without the discussions I had with moms and dads about parenting this young adult generation well, and with young adults themselves. I'm grateful for the time you gave, and for your vulnerability, often shared over a Chapters chai or a Coffee Cottage latte. My special thanks to Alli, Jazmine, Hannah, Hannah, April, Romare, Colin, Hannah, Abigail, Jennifer and Jennifer, Joel, Staci, Leslie and Leslie, Kim and Kim, Nancy, Francie, Ginger, Nicole, Polly, Jill, Maggee, Amy, Leah, Marie, Jakob, and many others.

My church community is definitely part of my village, and while working on this book, I often left Sunday worship with more ideas I wanted to include. We've attended North Valley Friends Church for five years now, and it feels more like home than any other church I've attended. My deepest gratitude especially goes to Leslie Murray, whose wisdom, thoughtfulness, and good humor keeps me grounded and inspires me to live with integrity and fearlessness and laughter. Let's climb a mountain again soon.

While completing this project, I met with several peer consultants in the Academic Resource Center (ARC) at George Fox University to talk about my book and to look at my drafts. Rick Muthiah and I started the ARC in 2003, and I truly believe it is a resource for *all* writers on our campus, not just those who struggle. My time at the ARC this past year reinforced this idea, and I'm especially grateful for the wisdom Abby Card and Hannah Lee gave me. They were both students at the university, and their insights shaped so much of this book. I especially appreciate the times they were honest with me about what I'd gotten wrong with their generation.

In addition to Abby and Hannah, I'm grateful for my students at George Fox University. Sharing their lives with me has been another unwarranted gift. In twenty-plus years, I've met some of the most astounding young people this world has to offer, and to name them all here would take another hundred pages, at least. Thank you all for making me the person God created me to be.

The Department of Language and Literature at George Fox informs so much of my life with young people, and I cannot imagine working with a wittier, kinder, more thoughtful group of colleagues. You've all made me a better writer and thinker, and your influence is threaded through my classroom and through what I've written here. In particular, I'm grateful for my chair, Gary Tandy, whose constant encouragement is also a gift.

Few people have influenced my parenting more than my little sister, Amy Landes. She had children earlier than me, and I've consistently looked to her for advice on how to parent well, especially now that our kids are young adults. Even if she's not named but once or twice in this book, her influence is everywhere in these words.

Finally, my family is at the heart of this book, and of my life. I'm grateful for my husband Ron; his support and his willingness to do things I dislike, from emptying the dishwasher to doing taxes, gave me more space to write. His unconditional love for me, and for his children, inspires me to want to be a better person. I'm grateful for my stepchildren Melissa and Ryan, and for the grandkids that Melissa and her spouse Rahul have provided. The support that Melissa, Rahul, and Ryan have offered their little brothers has been nothing short of miraculous, whether that support looks like a Zoom call or a safe place to land for a few days (or months).

This book couldn't have been written without the love and care of my sons, Benjamin and Samuel. I'm proud of the young men they are becoming out in the world, but I miss them every single day. Thank you both for all the ways you make this life better than I could have imagined.

NOTES

Introduction

1. I would love to read and discuss your reflections, even if I'm not grading your work. Feel free to send me your answers to these short assignments, and I will definitely respond!

Chapter 1

1. Frederick Buechner, *Listening to Your Life: Daily Meditations* (New York, Harper Collins: 1992), 289.

Chapter 2

1. Reece Johnson, "New Survey Finds Most College Grads Would Change Majors," BestColleges, November 11, 2021, https://www.bestcolleges.com/blog/college-graduate-majors-survey/.
2. See Frederick Buechner, *Wishful Thinking: A Seeker's ABC* (Harper Collins, 1993), 119. First published 1973.
3. Buechner, 119.
4. Anne Lamott, *Traveling Mercies* (Avon, 2000), 168.

Chapter 3

1. Sarah Aamodt, "Brain Maturity Extends Well Beyond the Teen Years," interview by Tony Cox, Tell Me More, NPR Science Broadcast, October 10, 2011, https://www.npr.org/templates/story/story.php?storyId=141164708.

2. Christina Fox, "How the Lament Speaks to Our Fears," *Place for Truth*, March 2016, https://www.placefortruth.org/blog/how-the-laments-speak-to-our-fears.

3. Howard Macy, *Rhythms of the Inner Life: Yearning for Closeness with God* (Eugene, OR: Wipf and Stock, 2016).

4. Megan McCarty Carino, "Share of Young Adults Living with Parents below 50 Percent Again, but Still Elevated," *Marketplace*, October 8, 2021, https://www.marketplace.org/2021/10/08/share-of-young-adults-living-with-parents-below-50-again-but-still-elevated/.

5. Melanie Springer Mock, "Pandemic, not Pomp and Circumstance," *Red Letter Christians*, April 17, 2020, https://www.redletterchristians.org/pandemic-not-pomp-and-circumstance/.

6. Eugene Peterson, *Leap Over a Wall* (New York: HarperOne, 1998).

7. Soong-Chan Rah, *Prophetic Lament: A Call for Justice in Troubled Times* (Westmont, IL: InterVarsity Press, 2015).

Chapter 4

1. Cited in Danielle Braff, "Why Does Loneliness Peak for Some Before Our 30s?," *Healthline*, last modified May 12, 2021, https://www.healthline.com/health/mental-health/loneliness-after-college.

2. See *Making Caring Common*, "Loneliness in America: How the Pandemic Has Deepened an Epidemic of Loneliness and What We Can Do about It," Harvard Graduate School of Education, February 2021, https://mcc.gse.harvard.edu/reports/loneliness-in-america; Eleanor Rees and Rebecca Large, "Coronavirus and Loneliness, Great Britain: 3 April to 3 May 2020," Office for National Statistics in Britain, June 8, 2020, https://www.ons.gov.uk/peoplepopulationandcommunity/wellbeing/bulletins/coronavirusandlonelinessgreatbritain/3aprilto3may2020.

Chapter 5

1. In Vietnam, a person's surname comes before their given name. Quan is my son's given name, though we are unsure who gave it to him, as well as his last name, Minh.

2. Melanie Springer Mock and Rebekah Schneiter, eds., *Just Moms: Conveying Justice in an Unjust World* (Newberg, OR: Barclay Press, 2011).

Chapter 7

1. Josh Packard, "Gen Z Is Turning Away from Religion in Order to Live Out Their Values," *Religion Dispatches,* November 5, 2021, https://religiondispatches.org/gen-z-is-turning-away -from-religion-in-order-to-live-out-their-values/.

2. Jeffery Jones, "US Church Membership Falls Below Majority for the Very First Time," Gallup, March 29, 2021, https://news .gallup.com/poll/341963/church-membership-falls-below -majority-first-time.aspx.

3. Barton Gingerich, "The Millennial Generation's Acceptable Sin," *Gospel Coalition*, January 7, 2013, https://www .thegospelcoalition.org/article/the-millennial-generations -acceptable-sin/. Data does not bear this out; in several surveys, young people are having less sex than previous generations.

4. Chrissy Stroop, "'Leaving to Sin' Is More About Evangelicals' Obsession with Sex," Flux, March 26, 2021, https://flux .community/chrissy-stroop/2021/05/leaving-christianity -religion-repression-desire/.

5. Yonat Shimron, "Young Adults Are Leaving the Church. LGBTQ Bias May Be Driving Them Away," Religion News Service, August 6, 2021, https://religionnews.com/2021/08/06/ young-evangelicals-are-leaving-church-resistance-to-lgbtq -equality-is-driving-them-away/.

6. Emma Green, "The Unofficial Racism Consultants to the Evangelical World," *The Atlantic*, July 5, 2020, https://www .theatlantic.com/politics/archive/2020/07/white-evangelicals -black-lives-matter/613738/.

7. Robert Jeffries, pastor of First Baptist Church in Dallas, Texas, called Donald Trump "the most Christian president" during

an interview with Fox News in June 2019, and supported the "godly" president through Trump's 2020 run for reelection.

8. See the Focus on the Family study series "Empowering Your Family to Face Critical Race Theory," with hosts Carol Swain and Danny Huerta, https://familyu.focusonthefamily.com/empowering-your-family-to-face-crt-episode-1/. I was directed to this series by journalist Kathryn Jones, "Evangelicals Do Battle with 'Critical Race Theory' in a New Online Video Course," *Salon*, January 15, 2022, https://www.salon.com/2022/01/15/evangelicals-do-battle-with-critical-race-theory-in-new-online-video-course/.

9. Matthew Impelli, "Student's Online Comment about 'Auctioning Off Black Classmates' Sparks Investigation," *Newsweek*, September 15, 2021, https://www.newsweek.com/students-online-comment-about-auctioning-off-black-classmates-sparks-investigation-1629503.

10. Brea Perry, "To the Pastors of the TikTok Generation," *The Witness*, January 19, 2022, https://thewitnessbcc.com/to-the-pastors-of-the-tiktok-generation/.

11. Emily Joy Allison, *#ChurchToo: How Purity Culture Upholds Abuse and How to Find Healing* (Minneapolis: Broadleaf Books, 2021).

12. Robert Downen, Lise Olsen, and John Teseco, "Abuse of Faith," *Houston Chronicle*, February 10, 2019, https://www.houstonchronicle.com/news/investigations/abuse-of-faith/.

13. Ruth Graham and Elizabeth Dias, "Southern Baptist Sex Abuse Stuns, from Pew to Pulpit," *New York Times*, May 23, 2022, https://www.nytimes.com/2022/05/23/us/southern-baptist-sex-abuse-report.html.

Chapter 8

1. Emetophobia sounds weird, but it can be paralyzing. It shows up on many "top ten phobia" lists, and has a high prevalence of sufferers. At least 8 percent of the adult population has emetophobia, according to one study.

2. John Della Volpe, *Fight: How Gen Z Is Channeling their Fear and Passion to Save America* (New York: St. Martins, 2021), 15.

3. Volpe, 18–19.

4. On "zombies," see Jeremy S. Adams, "The Rise of the Zoombies: Lifeless, Detached Students Have Returned to My Classroom," *LA Times*, July 24, 2021, https://www.latimes.com/opinion/story/2021-07-24/zoom-classroom-detached-students; quotation from Jeremy Adams, *Hollowed Out: A Warning about America's Next Generation* (Washington, DC: Regnery, 2021), 2.

5. Christina Caron, "What Gun Violence Does to Our Mental Health," *New York Times*, May 28, 2022, https://www.nytimes.com/2022/05/28/well/mind/gun-violence-mental-health.html.

6. Júlia Ledur, Kate Rabinowitz, and Artur Galocha, "There Have Been 300 Mass Shootings So Far in 2022," *Washington Post*, July 5, 2022, https://www.washingtonpost.com/nation/2022/06/02/mass-shootings-in-2022/.

7. Volpe, 99.

8. Dave Gilson, "You Can't Understand White Supremacy without Looking at Masculinity," *Mother Jones*, July/August 2018, https://www.motherjones.com/politics/2018/07/men-white-racist-extremism-michael-kimmel/.

9. Luis Noe-Bustamente et al., "About a Third of Asian Americans Say They Have Changed Their Daily Routine due to Concerns over Threats, Attacks," Pew Research Center, May 9, 2022, https://www.pewresearch.org/fact-tank/2022/05/09/about-a-third-of-asian-americans-say-they-have-changed-their-daily-routine-due-to-concerns-over-threats-attacks/.

10. John Woolman, *The Journal of John Woolman*, Christian Classics Ethereal Library, 27–28. First published 1774. Available at https://www.ccel.org/ccel/w/woolman/journal/cache/journal.pdf.

11. Anne Lamott, "I Don't Want to See a High School Football Coach Praying at the 50-Yard Line," *New York Times*, July 8, 2022, https://www.nytimes.com/2022/07/08/opinion/prayer-supreme-court-football.html.

12. Gabrielle Abdelmessih, "Gen Z Is Done with Just 'Thoughts and Prayers,'" *Oakland (Univ.) Post*, June 15, 2022, https://oaklandpostonline.com/42772/showcase/letter-from-the-editor-gen-z-is-done-with-just-thoughts-and-prayers/.

13. Quoted in Nikki Rojas, "Mass Shootings Reignite Youth Gun Control Push," *Harvard Gazette*, June 8, 2022, https://news.harvard.edu/gazette/story/2022/06/deadly-mass-shootings-reignite-youth-gun-control-push/.

14. Ian Ward, "Inside the Progressive Movement's TikTok Army," *Politico*, March 27, 2022, https://www.politico.com/news/magazine/2022/03/27/progressive-gen-z-for-change-tik-tok-00020624.

15. Hannah Getahun, "She Helped Raise $2 Million for Abortion Funds by Calling Out Matt Gaetz," *Business Insider*, August 27, 2022, https://www.businessinsider.com/olivia-julianna-abortion-fundraiser-trolled-matt-gaetz-2-million-dollars-2022-8.

THE AUTHOR

Melanie Springer Mock is professor of English at George Fox University,
an evangelical Friends institution in
Newberg, Oregon, where she primar-
ily teaches first-year writing, memoir, and journalism
courses. She is author or coauthor of six books, including
Worthy: Finding Yourself in a World Expecting Someone Else
(Herald Press, 2018). Her essays and reviews have appeared
in *Ms. Magazine, The Nation, Christian Feminism Today,
Chronicle of Higher Education, Runner's World,* and *Inside
Higher Education,* among other places, and she is a regular
reviewer for *Anabaptist World, Red Letter Christians,* and
Christians for Social Action.

She and her husband live in Dundee, Oregon, and have
two young adult sons. She is a stepmom to two adults, and
"Nani" to two grandsons. In her free time, Melanie enjoys
running, swimming, biking, knitting, and watching reality
television.